Informationsmanagement in Theorie und Praxis

Reihe herausgegeben von
A. Gadatsch, Sankt Augustin, Deutschland
D. Schreiber, Sankt Augustin, Deutschland

Das Informationsmanagement steht im Spannungsfeld zwischen betriebswirtschaftlichen und technischen Herausforderungen. Aktuelle Themen wie Digitalisierung, Big Data und die sich hieraus entwickelnden disruptiven Geschäftsmodelle spiegeln sich in starken Veränderungen wieder, sowohl in der Theorie, als auch in der Praxis. Die Schriftenreihe „Informationsmanagement in Theorie und Praxis" greift diese Themen auf, sowohl in der Forschung in Form herausragender Dissertationen, als auch in der Umsetzung durch exzellente Masterarbeiten.

Information Management is located between business and technical challenges. Current topics such as Digitalization, Big Data and the resulting disruptive business models are reflected in strong changes, both in theory and in practice. The series "Information Management in Theory and Practice" sets a focus on these topics, both in research theses (Ph. D.), as well as in practice theses (MSc).

Weitere Bände in der Reihe http://www.springer.com/series/16088

Anne Dreller

Creating Value from Data Sharing

Future-oriented Business
Models in Theory and Practice

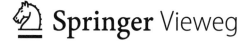 Springer Vieweg

Anne Dreller
Köln, Germany

With many thanks to Prof. Dr. Andreas Gadatsch (Hochschule Bonn-Rhein-Sieg), Prof. Dr. Dirk Schreiber (Hochschule Bonn-Rhein-Sieg), Bastian Schütz (Cofounder Quemey GmbH), Dennis Fleischer (Cofounder Quemey GmbH), inasys GmbH, and itemis AG

ISSN 2524-4205 ISSN 2524-4213 (electronic)
Informationsmanagement in Theorie und Praxis
ISBN 978-3-658-23275-7 ISBN 978-3-658-23276-4 (eBook)
https://doi.org/10.1007/978-3-658-23276-4

Library of Congress Control Number: 2018952471

Springer Vieweg
© Springer Fachmedien Wiesbaden GmbH, part of Springer Nature 2018

This Springer Vieweg imprint is published by the registered company Springer Fachmedien Wiesbaden GmbH part of Springer Nature
The registered company address is: Abraham-Lincoln-Str. 46, 65189 Wiesbaden, Germany

Contents

List of Figures

List of Tables

List of Abbreviations[1]

3D	Three-dimensional
AG	Aktiengesellschaft (Stock Company)
API	Application Programming Interface
APM	Action Priority Matrix
BI	Business Intelligence
BM	Business Model
BMC	Business Model Canvas
CD	Compact Disk
CEO	Chief Executive Officer
CRM	Customer Relationship Management
CX	Customer Experience
DIY	Do It Yourself
EDI	Electronic Data Interchange
ERP	Enterprise Resource Planning
ExO	Exponential Organization
GmbH	Gesellschaft mit beschränkter Haftung (Limited Company)
HR	Human Resources
ICT	Information and Communication Technology
IFEC	Inflight Entertainment and Connectivity
IoT	Internet of Things

---

[1] Proper nouns, brand names and the like were deliberately excluded, since they are discernible from their description in the text.

IT	Information Technology
LC	Lean Canvas
NGE	Next Generation Enterprise
PoC	Proof of Concept
PVC	Platform Value Canvas
SaaS	Software as a Service
SCM	Supply Chain Management
USP	Unique Selling Proposition

Abstract

We observe massive technological progress in our global environment. It exerts tremendous transformative power on all aspects of private and business life, in which data play an increasing and outstanding role – especially for our economy. Great value is assumed to be inherent in data, but only extractable if the respective data are interpreted and brought into context. This implies the critical precondition of data access. And here, data sharing enters the stage.

The present project aims at answering the research question how future-oriented business models (BM) can look like that create value from data sharing. Such a BM will exemplary be developed for the startup Quemey[2] in a pragmatic and realistically feasible way. Currently, Quemey pursues the idea that air passengers can make better use of their flight time when participating in rewarded surveys, generating data that are valuable to companies of all kinds. For the future, their vision is to build a data sharing ecosystem across the entire travelling value chain, where all operators share their data to jointly unleash new and more value.

After analyzing related studies on data sharing, a multi-method research design compiles the scientific methodologies of a case study, a platform-oriented BM framework, customer interviews with a subsequent online survey, a scenario analysis and expert interviews, evaluated with the help of qualitative content analysis. Various resulting findings are then puzzled together, leading to Quemey's future-oriented BM, including implementation advice and prioritized next steps.

Whilst in literature it is beyond doubt that data sharing offers huge advantages, especially in research for the progress of science, the business world has not fully recognized and operationalized this fact yet. Quemey's case confirms this: even though its empiric validation showed a high user acceptance for their survey idea, they are confronted with many challenges

---

[2] Whenever Quemey is concerned and no explicit sources are indicated, the respective contents derive from the author's own thoughts or backgrounds from previous talks to Quemey's founders.

for their data sharing vision. The recommendation is to overcome these by offering strong values, growing their business into a powerful monopolist position, and eliminating interfering influences of technological, contractual and legal uncertainties or data privacy concerns.

1 Introduction

1.1 Problem Definition

Customers are a company's key asset – this is commonly accepted as one of the most important principles in management theory. But beyond a pure understanding, the conversion of this paradigm into actions is required: companies need to orientate all their decisions and actions towards their customers. In the past, the business world was rather concerned about making money, following a simple, commonly approved formula: *"Create a product or service, sell it, and collect money"* (Gansky, 2010, S. 5). But a significant change has prevailed since the bursting of the internet bubble: relationship management has gained focus (Cole, 2010, S. 86). Not a high sales performance in the immediate present, but sustainably satisfied and loyal customers are the capital of each (trading) company (Cole, 2010, S. 105). In view of dramatically increasing rivalry for the customers' favour, companies need to stand out from the mass of competitors with an exceptional customer experience (CX). Those who want to win and bind customers have to identify their needs even before customers themselves are aware of them (Abolhassan, 2016, S. 17), and they have to recognize and solve important problems (Johnson, 2010, S. 26).

Simultaneously, new forms of generating value for customers emerge. Companies enter customer relationships that comprise more than the plain exchange of products for money (Cowden, 2013, S. 177). A new model of network companies is rising, giving customers new choices, tools and information – resulting in their activation, meaning customers take part in the interaction (Gansky, 2010, S. 5) and even become prosumers in participative systems (Cole, 2010, S. 103).

Digital technologies are a critical precondition for both described aspects: they empower companies to draw important findings from customer data to offer tailored, compelling products and services. Going even further, the entire company-customer-interaction can thereby be designed in the most pleasant and comfortable way, according to the customers' preferences. This causes a feeling of true caring and honest attention (Gansky, 2010,

© Springer Fachmedien Wiesbaden GmbH, part of Springer Nature 2018
A. Dreller, *Creating Value from Data Sharing*, Informationsmanagement in Theorie und Praxis, https://doi.org/10.1007/978-3-658-23276-4_1

S. 95). On top of that, companies can create new and better values with digital technologies (Rogers, 2017, S. 17).

"*Still, the collection and use of consumer data is in its infancy*" (Gansky, 2010, S. 84). In this, the recently founded startup Quemey saw their opportunity: Quemey translated the immense value of customer data into their business idea. They developed the first solution worldwide which offers passengers on board of aircrafts a service for answering surveys, in order to make better use of all the waiting time during air journeys. In return, they get rewarded with incentives (Schütz & Fleischer, Quemey Company Profile, 2017, S. 6). With their concept, Quemey established the first market research channel in airplanes. At its core, their service is a Software as a Service (SaaS) solution, empowering airlines or market research enterprises to develop and manage surveys on board of airplanes, enabled by WiFi through Hot Spots (Schütz, Interview: Praxisprojekt zu Deinem Startup, 2017, S. 1). In Quemey's current business model (BM), they address the needs of multiple stakeholder groups (Schütz & Fleischer, Quemey GmbH. Introduction Emirates, 2017, S. 3): passengers who are entertained and rewarded during flights, airlines that want to better understand their customers to increase the average revenue per passenger, avionic partners that want to integrate Quemey into their systems or market research companies that want access to the encapsulated target group of air passengers.

So far, Quemey could win partners like Deutsche Telekom AG (DTAG), Virgin Atlantic, GfK (Gesellschaft für Konsumforschung) or LinkedIn, and first proofs of concept (PoC) were conducted successfully. But they envisage an even greater long-term vision: on top of the data from inflight surveys, they want to create a data sharing ecosystem along the entire travelling value chain – from leaving home until reaching the target destination (Schütz, Interview: Praxisprojekt zu Deinem Startup, 2017, S. 1). Along this chain, all involved service providers grant the others access to their data base. The idea is to increase the value of customer information by raising the amount of data that are combined. Finally, the combination of multiple data sources allows for additional insights, convertible into even more success-promising economic actions.

To turn this vision into reality, Quemey needs to refine their current BM. They need to come up with a concrete plan how to build up a large, connected data pool based on a data sharing ecosystem. Resulting from this, the primary research question for the present analysis is defined as follows: **how can a future-oriented BM look like, that creates new values from data sharing?**

1.2 Overarching Goal

According to Eric Ries, a startup is *"a human institution designed to create new products and services under conditions of extreme uncertainty"* (Ries, 2011, S. 8). Quemey meets this definition in each of dimension, as they build up a new SaaS solution in an environment of exponential change – with the only constant being a continuously accelerating rate of change (Diamandis, 2017, S. VII). The uncertainty resulting from this can be described by different risks, which are commonly distinguished into technology, market and implementation risk. Each startup is challenged to figure out how their addressed core problem can be approached with an appropriate BM at the lowest risk possible in each category (Ismail, Malone, & Van Geest, 2014, S. 120). This also counts for the exemplary examined startup Quemey: since their foundation, they have aspired to realize the idea of inflight surveys, for air passengers to make better use of their most valuable resource – time – and for Quemey to convert the collected data into value. But as stated above, Quemey aims for more in the long run. Their future vision is to create a huge data sharing model with all parties along the travelling value chain involved.

To realize this major goal, a new and refined BM is required. Hence, regarding the **"What"** this project shall deliver, it shall develop a next-level BM for Quemey. More precisely, it shall draw up a future-oriented BM design that resonates with their aspired data sharing approach and thereby answers the posed research question. Numerous questions come to mind which should be answered when thinking about this goal: Does Quemey address a relevant customer problem with their current approach of providing a survey service to make better use of waiting time for passengers travelling by plane? Which additional value would emerge from data sharing with other partners along the travelling value chain – for both partners and passengers? Why would other parties join this partnership? How can such a platform ecosystem be built up and monetized? To narrow this wide range of questions down to the most significant points, and as the term "business model" represents a very broad subject area, a certain topic limitation in terms of relevant components is required, which will be given later.

Regarding the question "**How**" this overarching goal shall be achieved, a pragmatic and realistically feasible solution shall be offered. The approaches which are to be developed shall be transferrable to business practice afterwards, to help Quemey to make their next steps. Hence, a pragmatic and feasible BM design is to be created, rather than a complex, highly sophisticated or academic one.

This aspect takes up the implementation risk from above: it is one thing to develop a new business strategy (or BM in this case), but it is another to actually operationalize a strategy into concrete measures and to successfully implement it in all its dimensions, in order to thrive (Holstein & Campell, 2009, S. 57). Whilst strategy development is mainly a thinking process, strategy execution is rather about action, but both is critical for success. To date, these two processes were usually understood as separate and sequential activities. But as both components go hand in hand, a feasibility check regarding execution should be anchored in the design phase already (Scheuss, 2016, S. 287).

Several execution barriers can impede the effective and efficient realization of strategic orientations, as e.g. compiled by Kaplan and Norton with the barriers of understanding, people, resource allocation and management learning (Niven, 2002, S. 9), or by Holstein and Campell with the issues of complexity, relying on wrong indicators, unbalanced focus, a time lag when implementing measures, and underestimating implementation as permanent process (Holstein & Campell, 2009, S. 59-60). To overcome all these implementation challenges and pay sufficient attention to the actual execution readiness of the developed BM, the focus on implementation shall be maintained rigorously in this analysis, in line with the described mind-set that execution thoughts must be embedded in design already.

1.3 Approach

Having defined this overarching goal, the natural next stage is to determine which steps lead to its accomplishment. According to Ash Maurya, a startup characteristically passes three different stages. The first one is always about identifying and defining a problem worth solving (Maurya, Running Lean. Iterate from Plan A to a Plan That Works, 2012, S. 8). In this spirit, the following research project starts its **introduction** with a problem definition that structures the core problem and aggregates it into a research question. From this, the overarching goal is derived, both on content and meta level. Next, a detailed action plan can be developed. This is what the present section does.

As a whole, this project consists of two parts. Part one assesses the topic from a theoretical viewpoint, part two applies these findings to the real business world by investigating the startup Quemey in a case study.

Looking at the **theory section**, relevant terms and definitions have to be specified first, in order to assure a common understanding. Having laid this foundation, a classical literature analysis will examine existing findings which are relevant for the overarching research question, dealing with data sharing and platform-based BMs in particular. After discussing basic concepts, the current status of data sharing will be studied from research perspective, and mirrored against examples from business practice. Next, a section on methodology delineates the tools and instruments which are chosen for the Quemey case study later on, namely case studies, business modelling frameworks, customer interviews and surveys, scenario analyses and expert interviews.

It then follows part two: the **case study**. To be able to dive deeper into the matter, a brief company introduction on Quemey will be given in the beginning. Afterwards, their current BM will be sketched. But in addition to a pure description, it will also be evaluated. Coming back to the three stages each startup passes according to Maurya, stages one (problem/ solution fit: do we have a problem worth solving?) and two (product/ market fit: have we built something that people actually want?) shall be checked (Maurya, Running Lean. Iterate from Plan A to a Plan That Works, 2012, S. 8). To testify a basic user acceptance as precondition for a successful business, (qualitative) customer interviews with air passengers and a more quantitatively designed customer survey will be run, in line with Maurya's problem and solution interviews from Running Lean (Maurya, Running Lean. Iterate from Plan A to a Plan That Works, 2012, S. 81-94) (Maurya, Running Lean. Iterate from Plan A to a Plan That Works, 2012, S. 95-110). Ultimately, also current challenges for Quemey shall be derived from this, supplemented with expert interview findings extracted by qualitative content analysis.

Especially in dynamic environments, strategic thinking means to observe the evolution of relevant influence factors, taking into account what could happen, which chances could be exploited or which actions seem most promising (Scheuss, 2016, S. 37). In this context, a scenario analysis shall forecast the most relevant future influence factors on Quemey's BM. Similar to the current challenges, expert interviews amend these future perspectives, based on which – accompanied by the other outlined findings – a future-oriented BM for Quemey can finally be deduced. This is the centrepiece of all considerations, and it shall conclusively answer its research question of how future-oriented BMs could look like that generate new values from data sharing.

To round the entire discussion off, a **conclusion** will draw an overall summary of the obtained findings. Also a critical reflection will be conducted, to scrutinize whether all scientific requirements and posed goals could be met. Finally, an outlook into the future will be given, as well as on further consequential opportunities for research. Figure 1 provides a graphical visualization of this action plan.

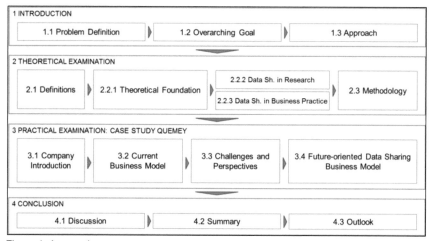

Figure 1: Approach
Source: own representation of the author

2 Theoretical Examination

2.1 Definitions

2.1.1 Data, Information and Knowledge

Before entering into further details, it is first necessary to clarify the most central terminology. As stated above, **data** depict the core of all considerations in this analysis. Data are commonly defined as a set of characters, which are compiled according to certain rules (syntax). In the next step, **information** are understood as data which are embedded in the context of a certain meaning (semantics). Finally, connected information, aiming at the generation of new findings, lead to **knowledge** (Clement & Schreiber, 2016, S. 28). This triad of data - information - knowledge is common ground and applied by many other researchers (Ferilli, 2011, S. 5) (Hinrichs, 2002, S. 27) (Zins, 2007, S. 479), even though the relations between these three concepts as well as their meanings are debatable (Zins, 2007, S. 479-485). In essence, this characterizes data as enabler for knowledge generation, since data which are enhanced by meaning result in information, and connected information then constitute knowledge (Clement & Schreiber, 2016, S. 28). At the same time, this supports the conclusion that generating knowledge is the ultimate objective and highest level of information productivity (Septer, 2013, S. 49), which requires to gather interpretable data that can be put into context. Nonetheless, the terms data and information are oftentimes used synonymously.

The **meaning of data** is usually described in many different ways depending on domain and author, but in summary it is beyond doubt that it is exceptionally high. Tenopir et al. for example state *"data are the infrastructure of science. Sound data are critical as they form the basis for good scientific decisions, wise management and use of resources, and informed decision-making"* (Tenopir, et al., 2011, S. 7). Leaving science and turning towards business practice, digital and information goods exert heavy influence on all aspects of today's social and economic life, often called information or knowledge society. Further, information (or knowledge) are meanwhile

© Springer Fachmedien Wiesbaden GmbH, part of Springer Nature 2018
A. Dreller, *Creating Value from Data Sharing*, Informationsmanagement
in Theorie und Praxis, https://doi.org/10.1007/978-3-658-23276-4_2

considered to be the fourth production factor, next to the classical production factors labour, land and capital (Clement & Schreiber, 2016, S. 32). Or, in other words, data are considered the raw material of our digital economy (Höttges, 2016, S. 1), revealing their full value when transformed (Gansky, 2010, S. 34), e.g. in information that are applied in a beneficial way.

In addition to that, data or information can also be responsible for fundamentally disruptive movements. Looking at today's economic world, which is more and more competitive, and which is driven by powerful megatrends like globalization, commoditization, and deregulation, companies are exposed to permanent change. Whether it be rapidly changing customer requirements, accelerating technological development or stronger competition – companies need to evolve and innovate or they are outperformed by new disruptive competitors (Moore, 2005, S. XIII-XIV). Whereas thousands of such disruptive changes can be observed worldwide, there is a substantial change from material carriers towards information carriers going on. This symbolizes that within these disruptive evolutionary leaps a fundamental change of the role of information takes place as well (Ismail, Malone, & Van Geest, 2014, S. 14). Everything can be supported or enabled by information, and thereby a reduction of marginal costs to almost zero can be realized. The search for new information sources that show potential to become the foundation for new companies and BMs are at the centre of the current Big Data revolution, offering new odds for business opportunities (Ismail, Malone, & Van Geest, 2014, S. 31). Ultimately, information-based products with marginal costs near zero combined with information-based externalization of business functions to customers can be considered responsible for a tremendous scalability of the respective BMs (Ismail, Malone, & Van Geest, 2014, S. 36). This very power of information is what drives Quemey, too: they rely on the power of information to create a disruptive, scalable BM.

2.1.2 Data Sharing

Consistent with this outstanding importance of data and information in general, the smooth flow of data is assumed to decide about business success in the future (Mühleck, 2016, S. 130). More precisely, enterprises (no matter of which size) can only unleash the full value of data when refining and transforming them. This requires access to data and hence data exchange as a fundamental precondition. The better this exchange works, the greater the realized value in the end (Mühleck, 2016, S. 136). And the better companies understand to collect data from different sources, to save them centrally, analyze and provide them to relevant applications in real-time, the better those data can serve to optimize CX, processes, innovations and operational as well as strategic decisions, as outlined in the introduction (Châlons & Dufft, 2016, S. 34).

Generally speaking, the data sources feeding the data inventory of a typical data warehouse can be categorized into internal and external sources (Bodendorf, 2006, S. 37). Internal ones provide e.g. data from operational systems the company runs their main processes with – external ones are typically situated outside the company, in the external environment, and relate to e.g. external data suppliers such as customers or partners. Whilst internal sources are under the sovereignty of the owning company (in both maintenance and access), external ones are not. Consequently, external sources need to grant the requesting company access to the desired data. This data exchange needs to be empowered by a certain exchange relationship between data supplier and data demander, which is often referred to as **data sharing**. Synonymously to data sharing, Paunovic describes data dissemination as *"the process of transfer of data between users"* (Paunovic, 2008, S. 199). In general, the sharing of data, information and knowledge is enabled by advanced information and communication technology (ICT), since data can be provided to various users almost in real-time via the internet for example (Paunovic, 2008, S. 201). Everything that can be connected, will be connected (Höttges, 2016, S. 5) – and by implication produce further data and empower their transfer. Simultaneously with these new possibilities from increased connectivity, the demand for data sharing is rising rapidly: more organizations either grant access to their own data or request access to other companies' data, to be able to generate value thereby (Son, Kang, Jo, Choi, & Lee, 2014, S. 452).

But even if data are available or accessible, this does not necessarily mean that these data are interpretable – it takes further effort to release their inherent value. Data are not only stored in different systems, they also have different formats, coming along as structured, semi-structured or unstructured data. Accordingly, appropriate ways must be found how to deal with this variety of different data sources (systems) and formats (Barbará & Clifton, 1993, S. 80). How can interoperability be assured? In 1993, Barbará and Clifton suggested to develop interoperation tools, but at the same time they stated that human intervention would be necessary to assure exhaustive environment interoperation (Barbará & Clifton, 1993, S. 81). With ongoing technological progress, human intervention may be reduced, and the fact remains that a (technological) solution is required to bridge the gap between incompatible data sources.

In this connection, the concept of **data or information broking** has established. A data broker can be compared with the role of a financial broker, who depicts the intermediary between different parties in an exchange relationship. According to Krumm et al., it empowers *"the seamless exchange of management data transactions"* (Krumm, Sabin, & Clark, 1999, S. 201), by allowing autonomous and heterogeneous data pools to arrange an information sharing process. Moreover, each side of the exchange relationship is only confronted and directly interacting with the broker, who is able to translate the individual input formats in neutral ones via an internal data base, running translation, storing and error recording. Afterwards, the broker forwards the neutral data to the other party. Altogether, the broker serves as problem solver for both sides, offering a list of advantages such as the elimination of multiple data entries and queries, system integration, interoperability with standard desktop applications, instant access to data, also via web-based technology, and others. All these aspects entail that huge cost and time savings can be realized (Krumm, Sabin, & Clark, 1999, S. 201-202).

To draw a conclusion of what was outlined above, data sharing is understood as the simple exchange relationship of transferring data between different parties, whilst data broking involves an intermediary between those parties, offering specific services to facilitate the participating parties to actually extract the value inherent in the exchanged data.

After all, not only the technological **prerequisites** for accessing and assuring interpretability are required, but also data sharing services themselves need to be specified (Son, Kang, Jo, Choi, & Lee, 2014, S. 452). This is related to the sum of all conditions and specifications which were partly sketched above, since there are many questions to be answered when entering a data sharing relationship. Which contractual conditions will apply? Which interface will empower the sharing process? Is a platform-based broker model required, to assure interoperability of different technologies and thereby interpretability of heterogeneous data? Or is it realistic that a cross-industry standard will prevail, providing general regulations on all these questions? In conclusion, this thread attests the need for a holistic data sharing BM, which will be taken up later.

2.1.3 Future-oriented Business Models

In the course of the startup boom in the 1990ties and when the internet economy had its golden period, the term „**Business Model**" has established as new notion in both scientific and popular scientific literature (Scheuss, 2016, S. 216) (Deelmann & Loos, 2003, S. 6). From then onwards, it has become more and more present and prevalent in the recent past, although no commonly accepted definition has prevailed so far, due to the term's diverse and varying utilization (Deelmann & Loos, 2003, S. 6). This holds true for both the context of science, looking at various different definitions by numerous authors, and business practice, meaning that even within the same company there can be multiple different understandings (Gassmann, Frankenberger, & Csik, 2013, S. 5) (Ematinger, 2018, S. 21). Hence, determining a definition as basis for the present project is even more important.

According to Scheuss, a BM can be understood as the concise description of one's business intention, the depiction of one's business strategy and the specific outlining of one's value-adding processes (Scheuss, 2016, S. 216). Other than that, Rogers states that BMs are composed by two main elements: a value proposition (focusing on the key value a company promises its customers) and a value network (describing all people, partners, assets and processes that are necessary to fulfil one's value proposition) (Rogers, 2017, S. 228). Another suggestion is given by Gassmann et al. who pose that a BM is characterized by the following questions: who are the customers, what is sold, how is it produced and how can earnings be realized – or in short by "who-what-how-value?" (Gassmann, Frankenberger, & Csik, 2013, S. 7).

All of these attempts at a definition interpret the process of finding a definition as the listing of different "ingredients" of a BM. Deelmann and Loos share this understanding, so their definition specifies a BM as the abstracting description of an organizational entity's normal business activities (Deelmann & Loos, 2003, S. 7). This abstraction can refer to graphical representations of organizational entities, transformation processes, transfer flows, influence factors or tools (Scheer, Deelmann, & Loos, 2003, S. 22). Deelmann and Loos argue their definition integrates different BM elements of other proposals, without restricting their understanding too much on a single or a group of BMs, e.g. eBusinesses (Deelmann & Loos, 2003, S. 7).

Nonetheless, even this integrated approach of Deelmann and Loos constitutes a definition that is based on a list of ingredients, entailing the risk of focusing on an arbitrary selection of relevant components, which might not be systematically selected. For this reason, the present project will choose a different understanding of BMs. Ematinger outlines that when asking executives for their understanding of a BM, they would probably give vague answers. Their answers would contain for example the company structure or processes rather than aspects about the fundamental logic of how the business works (Ematinger, 2018, S. 21). Ematinger's implicit thought of this fundamental logic how the business works is chosen as elementary understanding of a BM in this case. It does not focus on randomly selected elements, but on the main purpose and intention of a BM: it is about how the fundamental logic that determines how the business works in all relevant dimensions.

In line with this thinking, different categories of BMs are often distinguished. Greenberg et al. suggest discerning the three major groups of linear value chains (covering classical value-adding steps of "invent, produce, sell"), horizontal platforms (operating in a cross-industry model with own hard assets) and so-called "any-to-any" ecosystems like Uber, Alibaba or AirBnB (based on platforms but working with nearly zero own assets) (Greenberg, Hirt, & Smit, 2017, S. 45). Other than that, Gassmann et al. identified 55 BM patterns, like Crowd Funding/ Sourcing, Customer Loyalty, Layer Players, No Frills, Open Source, Reverse Innovation or White Label, to list a few examples (Gassmann, Frankenberger, & Csik, 2013, S. X-XIII). Again, this shows definitional variety when talking about BMs. Likewise, many different methods for visualizing BMs have developed. For the purpose of answering the overarching research question, choosing the right BM framework to elaborate it for the example of Quemey is paramount. Consequently, the discussion and selection of different frameworks will receive special attention in chapter 2.3.3.

Ultimately, it is to be clarified what **future-oriented** means as conceptual additive of this project's title. Amongst researchers and practitioners there is common agreement that BMs are of outstanding importance in today's time. Products, processes and services on their own are not capable of making a company successful. Future competition will rather be about BMs instead. Examples of the most successful and innovative companies of today prove that their prosperity is not based on great new products, but rather on their innovative overall BM: Amazon is the largest book retailer without a single retail store, Apple is the largest music retailer without having sold a single CD, Pixar won eleven Oscars in ten years without showing a single actor, Netflix reinvented the video library business without running a single video library themselves – the list could go on and on (Gassmann, Frankenberger, & Csik, 2013, S. 4-5). It shows without doubt that BMs underlie permanent change due to the rise of new digital technologies and disruptive threats, inverting traditional BMs. Hence, companies who want to stay successful in the new digital era need to think about BM innovation (Rogers, 2017, S. 7).

According to Christensen, successful BM innovations are realized by managers who develop and commercialize disruptive technologies, capable of developing or addressing new markets instead of conquering existing ones. Moreover, they plan to fail early and with low costs, whilst simultaneously creating new ways of working in their organization and transforming their value and cost structures in line with their disruptive vision (Christensen C. M., 1997, S. 99). Christensen's thoughts are extended by Ismail's vision of exponential organizations (ExO). To his mind, disruptive technology is only one driving force, among other influence factors like DIY innovators, crowdfunding, crowdsourcing or the "rising billion" of new consumers in Africa and Asia. All these factors in combination drive the constantly accelerating rate of change, with a new level of creative force. Ismail raises the question how this creative force can be used, and how companies can be created that are as agile, adaptive, innovative and fast as their employees (Diamandis, 2017, S. VII). His answer is the phenomenon of exponential organizations, being characterized by a disproportionately high return (at least ten times higher) compared to conventional organizations, due to the application of new organizational methods which are based on accelerating technologies. ExOs do not require huge amounts of workers or huge factories, as they rest on information technologies (IT) which transfer formerly material things into the digital world, where they are always available (Ismail, Malone, & Van Geest, 2014, S. 5).

Ismail et al. are not alone with their vision: there is a vivid discussion how the rapidly changing environment influences the design of future enterprises. Kishore and McLean label their vision "Next Generation Enterprise" (NGE), defined as a new, virtual organization that is based on the "*modern-day evolving pervasive and mobile information technologies*" (Kishore & McLean, 2002, S. 126). Although their concept is not a 100% congruent with the ExO concept, it focuses on the same elementary topics, declaring technological and organizational challenges responsible the future enterprise's shape (Kishore & McLean, 2002, S. 136).

Resulting from this train of thought, a future-oriented BM shall be under-stood as one that is potentially capable of growing into an ExO. This counts for both the development of a disruptive and scalable technology, and for the required companionship of an appropriate, also scalable organizational setting. It is understood as future-oriented because ExOs are capable of defining new industry paradigms and thereby securing to stay successful in a world that is changing faster than ever, whilst conversely, major indus-try giants fail, even though they are excellent at their core business.

2.1.4 Value Generation

The last remaining component of the present project's title is the aspect of **value generation**. It is treated as synonym to value creation in the follow-ing. In an economic consideration, a transaction can only take place if both the demand and the supply side see a chance that their individual expec-tations get fulfilled (Hoffmeister, 2015, S. 55). Hence, all parties need to recognize value in any transaction-based relationship (Walter, Ritter, & Gemünden, 2001, S. 366). Anderson agrees to this and explicitly labels this aspect as value creation, stating that the most fundamental purpose for entering a collaborative relationship is to profit from working together. Following from this, *"value creation and value sharing can be regarded as the raison d`être of collaborative customer-supplier relationships"* (Anderson, 1995, S. 348). Hindle describes value creation on a more ab-stract level as a company's foremost raison d'être, against which its suc-cess is evaluated (Hindle, 2008, S. 201). Christensen and Methlie join him in this opinion, as they qualify value creation as a firm's performance (Christensen & Methlie, 2003, S. 28).

As this shows, value can be regarded from different perspectives. Usually, customer value receives most attention, as this is a crucial element for a customer's buying decision. But at the same time, there is value created for the supplier, determined by both direct and indirect functions of cus-tomer relationships (Walter, Ritter, & Gemünden, 2001, S. 365). Other than that, a company generates market value, referring to the value that the stock market gives the company, or book/ accounting value, when the value captured in its balance sheet is concerned (Hindle, 2008, S. 201). In the same sense of a value-oriented strategy approach, with the primary objective of increasing the company value, one can also differentiate between shareholder and stakeholder value (Poeschl, 2013, S. 2-3). Poeschl outlines that within a shareholder-oriented management approach the overarching goal is maximizing the profitability of the shareholders' investments in the firm (Poeschl, 2013, S. 79). On the other hand, the stakeholder value approach postulates that a company is also responsible to meet the expectations of other internal and external groups exerting influence on the company with its commercial viability and its performance capability (Poeschl, 2013, S. 128).

Moreover, value is a dynamic element. It can change over time, forced by different trigger events, such as supplier located changes, customer located changes or environment located changes (Flint, Woodruff, & Fisher Gardial, 1997, S. 166). One example for supplier located changes can be the design of their BM, with its respective structure and relevance concerning customer expectations (Christensen & Methlie, 2003, S. 28). Flint et al. emphasize that companies (suppliers) have to understand how their customers' value awareness changes, in order to respond adequately and assure their loyalty (Flint, Woodruff, & Fisher Gardial, 1997, S. 174).

Following from all these aspects, value generation is conceived as multidimensional and dynamic concept in the present research project. At its core, it is about providing benefits to the other party in a commercial relationship, with this other party noticing the received beneficial effects. This definition deliberately excludes the customer-supplier limitation, because as it will turn out later in the case study part Quemey is active in a multisided market, since platform businesses go beyond pure customer-supplier relations. At the same time, this definition includes a certain subjectivity inherent in the individual understanding of values, to respect the fact that value is rated differently depending on the viewing angle.

All the thoughts outlined above hold true for a traditional business world, where physical goods are exchanged for money, to put it in simple terms. Subsequently, the logical next question is how **value creation in the con-**

text of the internet economy takes place, where transactions are performed online and virtually. Amit and Zott posit that existing theories of strategic management or entrepreneurship fail to explain value creation in eBusinesses exhaustively. Further, they claim that business processed over the internet offers new sources for value creation (Amit & Zott, 2001, S. 493), enabled by the characteristics of virtual markets. These include – to list a few examples – increased information availability, reduced transaction costs, dis-intermediation in broker models, or new ways of connecting transaction parties via re-intermediation (Amit & Zott, 2001, S. 495).

Hence, the formula for value generation is no longer *"create a product or service, sell it, and collect money"* (Gansky, 2010, S. 5). On the contrary, new models grow, with businesses based on the new possibilities of *"mobile, location-based capabilities, web and social network growth, changing consumer attitudes, and the historically understood market benefits of share platforms"* (Gansky, 2010, S. 5). Gansky calls these emerging group of businesses "Mesh", characterized by focusing on network-enabled sharing, and selling access instead of ownership, which allows to sell exactly the same good numerous times. And these numerous interactions with customers lead to numerous contacts, new opportunities, more sales and finally a stronger overall customer relationship (Gansky, 2010, S. 5-6). In essence, Gansky summarizes this as getting *"more real value for people by leveraging the Web as a sharing platform"* (Gansky, 2010, S. 6).

From the internet economy perspective, Gansky thereby describes her vision of two- and multisided markets. These are characterized by different groups of participants who influence each other regarding the usage and the value of the respective market. Both sides are indirectly connected, whilst this connection is shaped by an intermediary who coordinates and organizes the network by running a platform (Clement & Schreiber, 2016, S. 264). Additional value for the platform users results from direct and particularly indirect network effects. In their most simple form, positive indirect network effects mean that the number of participants on one side of the market determines the value for the other side, since e.g. a marketplace with more sellers offers a greater product variety and cheaper prices due to increased competition (Clement & Schreiber, 2016, S. 266-267). And exactly this is where Quemey comes into play: with their data sharing vision, as described later on in the case study part, they aim at generating additional and a novel kind of value, by operating an innovative, exponential platform BM. Now that all relevant terminology is explained, Figure 2 provides a compact summary of the specified definitions.

2.1.1
DATA are defined as a set of characters, which are compiled according to certain rules (syntax). INFORMATION are understood as data which are embedded in the context of a certain meaning (semantics). Connected information, aiming at the generation of new findings, lead to KNOWLEDGE. This is the ultimate goal of data processing. The MEANING OF DATA is described in multiple variants, but all in all it is rated exceptionally high for our future economy.

2.1.2
DATA SHARING is understood as the simple exchange relationship of transferring data between different parties. DATA BROKING involves an intermediary (data broker) between these parties, offering specific services to facilitate the participating parties to actually extract and utilize the value inherent in the exchanged data.

2.1.3
A BUSINESS MODEL's main purpose and intention is to define the fundamental logic that determines how the business works. A FUTURE-ORIENTED BM is understood as one that is potentially capable of growing into an exponential organization, both regarding the development of disruptive, scalable technology, and regarding an appropriate, also scalable organizational setting.

2.1.4
VALUE GENERATION is conceived as multidimensional and dynamic concept. At its core, it is about providing benefits to the other party in a commercial relationship, with this other party noticing the received beneficial effects. The rise of the INTERNET ECONOMY TRANSFORMS VALUE CREATION, offering additional and novel value creation possibilities by e.g. encouraging innovative, exponential platform businesses and other economic phenomena such as network effects.

Figure 2: Summary of Relevant Definitions
Source: own representation of the author based on the findings of 2.1.1, 2.1.2, 2.1.3 and 2.1.4

2.2 Related Studies

2.2.1 Theoretical Foundations

After creating a common understanding on relevant terminology, the concept of data sharing shall now be scrutinized from a theoretical point of view. First, data sharing will be explained in the light of different influence factors and frame concepts, to provide background knowledge on relevant theories. This acts as sound basis to later assess their current state in research and business practice.

According to Kim et al., the digital economy depicts one of the major and most crucial characteristics of the knowledge-based society which will surround us in the future. *"Based on information and communications technology (ICT), it grows faster than and eventually overtakes the traditional industrial economy"* (Kim, Kim, Park, & Hwang, 2014, S. 163). In essence, they declare exponential technological development responsible for the digital transformation of all aspects of life, both regarding economic implications and their impact on society. This outstanding, continuous and seemingly impossible development occupies many researchers in the recent past and even more today, as for example outlined by Ismail et al. in their ExO concept (Ismail, Malone, & Van Geest, 2014, S. 5).

One of the best-known perspectives on the **acceleration of technological progress** originates from futurologist Ray Kurzweil: in 2001, he developed the "Law of Accelerating Returns", stating that in contrast to our perceived "intuitive linear view" the historical development of technology proves that today's world is confronted with exponential technological change. In line with this thought, the 21st century will not bring 100 years of progress – it will rather bring 20.000 years of advancement in technology (Kurzweil, 2001, S. 1). Ismail et al. summarize Kurzweil's theories in the following four observations (Ismail, Malone, & Van Geest, 2014, S. 6):

First, the patterns of duplication as ascertained by Moore for the case of integrated circuits can be transferred to all kinds of IT. Kurzweil calls this the "Law of Accelerating Returns" – calculating that the duplication of computing power can be traced back until 1900, far more than assumed by

Moore himself. Second, a central driver for this phenomenon is information. As soon as a certain discipline, technology, area or industry is based on information and steered by such, its total performance is doubling every single year. Third: as soon as the patterns of duplication have started, they will not stop anymore, due to a self-enforcing effect: faster computers are used to build faster ones, leading to even much faster ones and so forth. And finally, as key technologies are based on information today, artificial intelligence, robotics, nano technology, medicine, neuro sciences, data bases and science or 3D printers etc. show the same effects.

From these thoughts, Kurzweil concludes that within a foreseeable amount of time – more precisely: within a few decades – machine intelligence will become more powerful than human intelligence (Kurzweil, 2001, S. 1). He baptized this phenomenon "Singularity" – meaning that in 2045, he expects all computers on earth together to be as powerful as all brains of all existing human beings (Zimmermann, 2017, S. 19). Never before in the history of humanity it was observable that so many technologies were emerging simultaneously at such a fast pace. And as they are combined and connected, they speed up innovations even further: each new connection unfolds as new multiplier (Ismail, Malone, & Van Geest, 2014, S. 6).

One important section of this technological development pertains to the topic of **data management**. New, scalable technologies allow to manage nearly exploding amounts of data, and to provide them in a stable, reliable, performant and secure way for their respective use cases (Abolhassan, 2016, S. 19). Physical objects are increasingly connected, continuously producing, processing and communicating new information – the physical world is more and more translated into data. New data-based BMs emerge (Châlons & Dufft, 2016, S. 28). And *"not only does the ICT-based digital economy affect the economic area, it also brings about all-round social change"* (Kim, Kim, Park, & Hwang, 2014, S. 167). Resulting from this, it must be asked whether humanity actually makes use of all the new, emerging possibilities that are provided, leveraging the value inherent in these masses of data and new data management supporting technologies. Is mankind even capable of understanding the full potential value from data and its consequences?

One prerequisite to actually unleash the value of data is to get access to the respective data. This is where **data sharing** comes into play. As examined in the definitions section (chapter 2.1.2), data sharing is understood as the process of transferring data between different parties. For this, companies (representing such parties) need to ensure they are able to collect data from different sources centrally, to save them, to evaluate them in real-time and to provide the right data to the right applications (Châlons & Dufft, 2016, S. 34). Or more precisely: at the right time, right quality, right amount, right location, and right recipient, as the logistics principle for information says (Augustin, 1990, S. 23-24). This counts for both cross-company data transfer, when different parties involved in a supply chain need to assure smooth information flows along their common process chains (Werner, 2017, S. 284), and for company-internal departments, to avoid inefficiencies resulting from silo structures (Gadatsch, 2012, S. 12-13).

From a supply chain management perspective, the exchange of data between commercial partners has been extensively discussed under the name of Electronic Data Interchange (EDI) yet. In this context, point-to-point linkages between suppliers (information sources) and customers (information drain) are established, to enable data exchange steered by e.g. requests, orders, invoices and the like. These system interfaces enable e.g. automated storage (Werner, 2017, S. 283). In total, Werner lists less redundancy in data collection, the reduction of manual activities, and the acceleration of communication processes as the main advantages resulting from EDI. On the other hand, he outlines critical aspects of cross-company EDI connections, which nonetheless do not contradict its virtues: High acquisition costs, intransparency regarding charges of network operators and the infringement of access rights in terms of secrecy (Werner, 2017, S. 284). Yu et al. agree with this view, highlighting the enormous benefits and hence the necessity of information sharing in supply chain management: the systematic coordination of all involved players along a value chain (or network) and the formation of partnerships *"creates a win-win situation for all members"* (Yu, Yan, & Cheng, 2001, S. 114). It results from improved business connections like vendor managed inventories, cross-docking warehouses and quick response, and the reduction of negative impacts from the so-called bullwhip-effect (Yu, Yan, & Cheng, 2001,

S. 114-115). Moreover, Yu et al. hypothesize that increased information sharing will cause Pareto-typical improvements for all parties involved along the entire implicated value chain, which they demonstrate with a modelling study and an analysis of different sharing levels (Yu, Yan, & Cheng, 2001, S. 118).

In general, data sharing is – as the name suggests – a form of sharing, meaning that it is to be considered in connection with the general **sharing economy** concept. The idea of the "shareconomy" (originally: "share economy") stems from Harvard economist Martin Weitzman, who developed it as a new cognitive model in reaction to the oil crisis in the 1970ies (Kraus & Giselbrecht, 2015, S. 79). He hypothesized that the wealth for market participants rises with an increasing level of shared goods and services amongst all participants, compared to the situation that each participant purchases and owns them separately (Goldhammer, 2013, S. 4). As this theory has spread, it is nowadays linked with many concepts and terms and *"has become a hot topic of many debates and economic interpretations"* (Bratianu, 2018, S. 3). In its original understanding, it embraces *"the sharing of objects, areas, property, knowledge, information and experiences between individuals"* (Kraus & Giselbrecht, 2015, S. 77). Consumers – especially from Generation Y – prefer access instead of ownership, particularly when recognizing attractive new products or services, which they want to use with lower personal and environmental costs (Kraus & Giselbrecht, 2015, S. 78) (Gansky, 2010, S. 5).

This trend of sharing in combination with changing customer preferences and behaviour (*"access rather than ownership"*, (Gansky, 2010, S. 5)) has evoked thousands of new ventures, which aim at providing their customers access to goods or services instead of following the conventional value creation model of developing, producing and selling goods (Gansky, 2010, S. 165). At the same time, they operate with new BMs. Gansky emphasizes a certain **pattern** that all these sharing BMs have in common: according to her "Mesh" businesses theory, these new ventures are based on platforms, and characterized by four central attributes (Gansky, 2010, S. 16). First, they offer something that is shared within a community, a market, a supply or value chain. Second, they are enabled by advanced web and mobile data networks that track goods and compile information about usage, customers and the product itself. As a third aspect, they focus on physical goods, as they make local delivery and recovery precious and appreciated. And fourth, they spread via word of mouth advertising, augmented by the power of social networks. These effects characterize platform BMs: whilst in the context of classical economic structures linear BMs provide customer benefits by the usage of the provided product or service itself, platform businesses provide benefits by the fact that the platform is used by other parties, too. In consequence, network effects emerge: the benefits for one market side are increased by the number of participants on the other market side. The platform itself has the role of a broker who orchestrates transactions between parties, who steers their transactions and who provides the required infrastructure and network (Walter M. , Plattform-Geschäftsmodelle verstehen und entwickeln, 2017, S. 15-16).

But the concept of sharing must not be limited to physical goods only. According to Richter, the categories of sharing goods, digital and intellectual content can be differentiated (Richter, Digital Collaboration and Entrepreneurship - The Role of Shareeconomy and Crowdsourcing in the Era of Smart City, 2016, S. 35). This is where data sharing can be allocated to, belonging to the category of digital content. Moreover, sharing is not restricted return-free sharing: it can be linked to both monetary and non-monetary benefits, as the definition by Richter et al. shows: "*shareconomy is an economic model enabled by modern ICT, (…) for monetary or non-monetary benefits*" (Richter & Kraus, The shareconomy as a precursor for digital entrepreneurship business models, 2015, S. 22).

To draw a conclusion from these theoretical considerations: the above notions from supply chain management indicate that from a technical point of view it is relatively easy to share data beyond an organization's boundaries. There might be obstacles to be overcome in each individual application case, but in total the enormous advantages of data sharing propose to make more use of it in practice, as outlined by the treatment of the shareconomy concept, too. At this point, the question remains whether these gains from data sharing are transferable to other contexts as well. Moreover: does society recognize the enormous impact of data sharing yet

– including all possible benefits for common wealth and monetization opportunities? Is there still room for more data sharing application cases, embedded into powerful platform BMs? And if so, which trends and success factors influence how data sharing is pursued? To answer these questions, the following two sections will outline the current status of data sharing first in research, and then in business practice with exemplary real-world businesses.

2.2.2 Data Sharing in Research

Generally speaking, there is a common body of opinion amongst researchers that knowledge **sharing is of outstanding importance for further scientific progress** and knowledge production (Stanley & Stanley, 1988, S. 178) (Tan, 2016, S. 525) (Son, Kang, Jo, Choi, & Lee, 2014, S. 447) (Van den Eynden, Corti, Woollard, Bishop, & Horton, 2011, S. 1). Many **advantages** are recognized, pleading for sharing research data to encourage new findings. Dehnhard for example compiles a long list of benefits resulting from data sharing: scientific progress, knowledge generation, transparency, openness, reanalysis, meta-analysis, replications, improvement and review of statistical methods, prevention of redundant data collection, application in education and others (Dehnhard, 2014, S. 58). Additionally, Mbuagbaw et al. see advantages regarding the promotion of fair and transparent clinical trials, and regarding the value maximization from data by permitting the investigation of additional hypotheses (Mbuagbaw, Foster, Cheng, & Thabane, 2017, S. 1). For all these reasons, data sharing is also attributed with an ethical meaning in research, particularly in medicine, where the treatment of serious diseases depends on medical advancement. In line with a rising ethical consciousness, data sharing is more and more considered an obligation for researchers rather than a voluntary activity or pure aspect of good collaboration (Stanley & Stanley, 1988, S. 173). Beyond that, van den Eynden et al. highlight increased visibility and impact of research, research promotion in combination with greater credit to the scientist, increased accountability and collaboration possibilities (Van den Eynden, Corti, Woollard, Bishop, & Horton, 2011, S. 3). Finally, data sharing can even be a prerequisite for funding (Van den Eynden, Write a Data Management and Sharing Plan, 2017, S. 5).

Even though these positive points are widely perceived and accepted as common view, there are many **problems and open questions** remaining that impede researchers from realizing a consequent sharing approach. Starting with a lack of definitional clarity and the respective guidelines (Sieber, 1988, S. 203), the pure handover act requires time and cost efforts from the sharing party. At the same time, there is often no appreciation for sharing, or even worse: it may lead to disadvantages in scientific competition. Moreover, researchers potentially become vulnerable as flaws of their research can be detected when opening up the underlying data base. Further, legal barriers such as data protection and copyright issues are a source of uncertainty, as there is too little knowledge about the legal situation and no exhaustive legal regulation (Dehnhard, 2014, S. 59).

Accordingly, scientists are discussing **how these challenges can be managed** in order to leverage the outlined benefits of knowledge sharing for the good of science. Van den Eynden summarizes the relevant actions to be taken under the critical precondition of assuring a *"good level of data management"* (Van den Eynden, Write a Data Management and Sharing Plan, 2017). At its core, data management comprises the activities of *"handling, housing, maintaining and preserving data"*, that help to assure high data quality, sound data organization and documentation, preservation, accessibility and controllable validity (Van den Eynden, Write a Data Management and Sharing Plan, 2017, S. 4). Of course, this also includes the necessary technological instruments for data sharing, such as an efficiently designed sharing platform (Son, Kang, Jo, Choi, & Lee, 2014, S. 447). Additionally, many authors emphasize other important aspects: Tan for example classifies relevant viewpoints which encourage data sharing into individual, organizational, technological and communication factors (Tan, 2016, S. 526). Other than that, Sieber sketches different data sharing cases, each presenting individual problems that are to be equipped with an appropriate solution (Sieber, 1988, S. 199).

Altogether, this analysis of data sharing in the academic context reveals: the enormous advantages and hence importance of data sharing amongst

researchers is commonly recognized and approved. Notwithstanding, turning this recognition into practice leaves room for improvement, even
though the outlined investigations present a first step in the right direction,
but many obstacles are still to be overcome. In essence, these obstacles
are less about technological issues (like providing technical access to the
respective data) but more about defining common standards, rules and
agreements on the conditions of data sharing. As recommended by Sieber
or Van den Eynden et al., researchers could encounter this issue by for-
ward-looking planning and by open dialogues and negotiations with their
sharing partners, to identify solutions that meet the interests of all involved
parties (Sieber, 1988, S. 206) (Van den Eynden, Corti, Woollard, Bishop,
& Horton, 2011, S. 6).

2.2.3 Data Sharing in Business Practice

As outlined above, data sharing in research is typically associated with an
ethical commitment of the researcher to contribute to scientific progress –
for the good of humanity, if you will. Leaving research and turning towards
the business world, there are other motivational structures influencing the
actions of the involved players. Against this background, a **different mind-
set** regarding open data sharing with e.g. competitors is the logical consequence and will be investigated in the following. Moreover, concrete examples of companies that actively pursue data sharing shall help to point out
characteristics, limitations and success factors.

Economic entities usually follow the economic principle. In its origin, the
economic principle describes the rational usage of existing resources in
order to maximize a company's profit (Schaumberger, 2011, S. 1). This
idea descends from the economic theory of the homo oeconomicus, who
is characterized by rational behaviour and the pursuit of individual benefit
maximization (Piekenbrock & Hennig, 2013, S. 23). Thus, economists
would rather not ask how they can contribute to the greater good, but would
instead wonder how to maximize their own advantages. This mind-set then
drives their actions – also concerning data sharing.

Therefore, it is not surprising that data sharing in business is not discussed as extensively as in the research context. Typically, companies only start to think about this matter when it is necessary for their BM or when they see relevant benefits for their business. This is why data sharing considerations normally start with concrete use cases that promise **relevant advantages**.

One such application area is supply chain management, as sketched in chapter 2.2.1. Yu et al. for example state that "*the power of information technology can be harnessed to help supply chain members establish partnerships for better supply chain system performance*" (Yu, Yan, & Cheng, 2001, S. 114). They substantiate their hypothesis with concrete advantages of sharing information with supply chain partners, such as reduced levels of inventory or cost savings, or even increased supply reliability (Yu, Yan, & Cheng, 2001, S. 114) (Yu, Yan, & Cheng, 2001, S. 119). Especially the aspect of uncertainty regarding demanded quantities along the chain can be encountered by strategic information exchange between partners (Yu, Yan, & Cheng, 2001, S. 114-115). Technically, EDI has established to process the exchange of data between different parties using defined interfaces. It contains a communication element, responsible for the physical transfer of data, and a conversion element, assuring the compatibility of data formats (Werner, 2017, S. 283). This dichotomy addresses two main aspects of data sharing: the question of accessibility and the prerequisites for interpretability, here: evaluable data formats.

Turning to a broader perspective, Baan and Homburg contemplate the topic of information sharing against the background of information productivity, being an expression for the value that the use of information contributes to a company's overall profitability. According to their analysis, and supported by other studies, information and knowledge sharing can increase a company's information productivity and thus favour its financial situation (Baan & Homburg, 2013, S. 16). One of these studies found that exchanging standardized data in the context of enterprise information systems such as ERP (enterprise resource planning), SCM (supply chain management) and CRM (customer relationship management) systems re-

sult in positive impacts on eBusiness functions like online sales and purchases, product design, demand forecasting or resource management
(Mehrjerdi, 2010, S. 309). Another study outlines the importance of combining multiple data sources to fully unleash the potential of BI (business
intelligence) for improved decision making (Ranjan, 2008, S. 472).

On the contrary to these benefits from data sharing, there are also **barriers**. Eckartz et al. classify the obstacles of data sharing into technical, data
quality, ownership, privacy and economic issues. Especially privacy concerns are often mentioned as relevant for private organizations, but often
without naming concrete questions. This suggests a general uncertainty in
terms of legal regulations on data privacy. Moreover, Eckartz et al. highlight economic considerations as prominent viewpoint, since companies
fear to lose competitive advantages by opening up sensitive data to competitors (Eckartz, Hofman, & Van Veenstra, 2014, S. 255).

Nonetheless, the above explained positive aspects manage to motivate
more and more private organizations to pursue data sharing. Since data
and analytics in general exert massive pressure for change on the worldwide industry landscape, new market entrants with **data-focused BMs** mix
up traditional market structures (Gottlieb & Rifai, 2017, S. 3).These new
competitors understand how to make use of their data- and analytics-re-
lated activities in order to generate new profits by so-called data monetization. According to Gottlieb and Rifai, data monetization is becoming a differentiator, and it correlates with companies that show industry-leading
performance (Gottlieb & Rifai, 2017, S. 3-4). There are many examples for
well-known new giants such as Facebook, Google, or Amazon, which
make most of their revenue based on user data (Giese, 2017, S. 1).

Next to these large ones who managed to disrupt entire industries, there
are numerous smaller businesses emerging, operating in the sense of a
data-based platform business. Gansky lists various examples in the context of her "mesh" theory. The app "Waze" for example offers community-
based traffic and navigation services, empowered by crowdsourced maps
that indicate the current traffic situation in real-time (Gansky, 2010, S. 224)
(Waze, no release date specified, S. 1). Other than that, Flextronics col-
lects information about end consumers to identify suggestions on product

design changes for producers (Gansky, 2010, S. 144). Taxi Magic, a taxi dispatch service, demonstrates the power of partnerships by promoting safe journeys home after a long night out jointly with the beer brand Heineken (Gansky, 2010, S. 30). Groupon bundles customer interests as a buying platform, and forms partnerships with goods or service providers by assuring large order quantities, to offer best prices and inspiration for their users (Gansky, 2010, S. 30). Finally, Zipcar – originally a Carsharing company – recognized patterns from user data, indicating new business opportunities as basis for their partnership approach: Zipcar collaborates with food and wine, hotel and fitness companies to offer ancillary services such as traffic advice, reservations in recommended restaurants or event suggestions (Gansky, 2010, S. 12).

Altogether, Gansky outlines the massive set of opportunities from increasing amounts of connected information: they allow a company to delight their customers with *"irresistible, timely, and customized offers"* (Gansky, 2010, S. 41). Hence, the key challenge for these businesses is to leverage the required infrastructure to exploit the new opportunities of customer-specific personalization. *"Integrating information from your own and other systems allows companies to offer better service to a particular flavour of customer."* (Gansky, 2010, S. 110).

Some companies even make **data sharing their core BM**: they collect data and make money by selling their data to companies for which they are relevant. IOTA is one example: in 2017, they established a peer-to-peer marketplace for sharing sensor data, particularly regarding IoT (internet of things) use cases. This shall empower new possibilities of machine to machine communication, where systems can trade data with each other (Giese, 2017, S. 2). The enormous potential inherent in this kind of new data marketplaces is underlined by huge partners that IOTA foundation could win already: Accenture, Bosch or Fujitsu believe in the future of this model and its transformative power comparable to Bitcoin technology (Giese, 2017, S. 3). Remembering the definitional section, IOTA can be classified as typical information broker model. It depicts a future-oriented platform model, as IOTA is becoming orchestrator, not participant only: according to MIT Professors Van Alstyne and Parker, successful businesses are developing from participants to orchestrators of a market (Walter M. , Webinar Plattform Geschäftsmodelle als Königsdisziplin des IoT, 2017, S. 7).

Similarly, large corporates take their first steps towards building up new data pools and generating valuable findings by enhanced analytics capabilities. Telekom Innovation Laboratories for instance have established data analytics as focus topic, with the development of new BMs with companies from other industries as one of their main goals (Telekom Innovation Laboratories, 2017, S. 1).

Again, all these cases show that there is an increasing awareness of the advantageousness of data sharing in the business world. On the other hand, its practical realization reveals many open issues that require the definition of appropriate solutions. Whilst on the technological side there are usually methods and experiences existing to process data exchange via appropriate interfaces, evaluating and generating value from these data with the respective instruments is often more challenging (*"the value of data is in its transformation"* (Gansky, 2010, S. 34)). Notwithstanding, the creation of a respective commercial agreement on the conditions of data sharing usually flags even more open issues than the technological perspective. The identification of respective BMs calls for new thoughts that leverage the possibilities of the internet economy and platform market structures with new partnerships, as the presented example cases pointed out. Exactly this is what will be taken up in the case study part for the startup Quemey.

2.3 Methodology

2.3.1 Key Requirements

After basic theoretical foundations were discussed in the previous chapter, the following one depicts the bridge between theory and practice. Since the obtained theoretical findings shall be applied in the context of Quemey later on, the next step is to select and explain appropriate scientific methodologies for doing so. These shall provide a certain frame construction and guidance with which the global research objective can be reached in a structured and systematic way. Hence, **certain requirements for the selection of appropriate methodologies** shall now be deduced, which then help to specify the concrete research design.

According to Nordlund et al., design can be described as the mapping process of (societal) needs to the answer how they are met (Nordlund, Kim, Tate, Lee, & Oh, 2016, S. 216). Put simply, Park summarizes this relation as follows: *"Design is the interplay between 'what we want to achieve' and 'how we achieve it'"* (Park, 2007, S. 17). Originally for the domain of engineering, MIT Professor Nam Pyo Suh developed the design framework of **Axiomatic design** to cope with this challenge. However, it is not limited to engineering, but applicable to all kinds of design endeavours (Park, 2007, S. 17), also in other disciplines (Foley & Harðardótti, 2016, S. 240).

Suh outlines the need for a systematic design approach by stating that many design mistakes can be traced back to a design process conducted in a trial-and-error mode (Suh, 2001, S. 2). Hence, Suh intended to convert design from an art into a more scientific activity, by identifying key characteristics that differentiate good from bad designs (Foley & Harðardótti, 2016, S. 240). In doing so he identified two axioms which are central to theory. Since axioms, originated from geometry, can by definition not be proven themselves, but revised when a counterexample is confirmed, one could argue that Suh's theories are somehow heuristic. Nonetheless, there was no opposite example detected yet, and many good designs could even be validated against this backdrop (Park, 2007, S. 17). In detail, axiom one is the axiom of independence, suggesting that interdependencies between functional requirements (user needs) should be reduced to a minimum. This allows for more flexibility in optimizing its elements when e.g. user needs change. As functional requirements are typically interlinked, it might be necessary to exchange others as well if one requirement is modified. Axiom two postulates that a good design is characterized by a minimal amount of information (Foley & Harðardótti, 2016, S. 241). In other words, this means a greater amount of overlaps between the design range (*"who it should impact*") and the operating range ("*who it does impact*") (Foley & Harðardótti, 2016, S. 243).

Transferring Suh's Axiomatic Design theory to the present case, a comparable but simplified approach shall be pursued. Hence, the challenge is to formulate a set of key design principles with which an appropriate research design can be determined, to bridge the gap between functional requirements (contributing to the overarching research goal) and design parameters (concrete requirements towards chosen scientific methods). As a result, the following **key design principles P1-P5** can be determined based on the overarching research objective, referring to either its "what" or its "how" dimension as illustrated in chapter 1.2.[3] It is assumed that if all selected methodologies meet these requirements, the findings they bring will do so either:

(P1) First and foremost, all chosen methodologies must **lead to relevant insights** regarding the overarching research question of how future-oriented BMs that generate value from data sharing could look like ("what" dimension).

(P2) As the answer to this question shall be found in a pragmatic way, the chosen methodologies shall **not be overwhelmingly complex,** to avoid spending too much effort on meta work, and to rather be able to put more focus on content ("how" dimension).

(P3) Pragmatic does also include that **easily understandable** methodologies are preferred, instead of highly sophisticated ones, as the developed solution shall be transferable to business practice afterwards. Nonetheless, the fundamental standards of scientific work shall be complied at all times ("how" dimension).

(P4) Regarding the feasibility of the developed concept, it is important to have room for adaptation, to react to unexpected changes appropriately. Hence, all methodologies need to be **flexible** for customization ("how" dimension).

---

[3] "what": delivering relevant insights regarding research question (primary goal); "how": doing so in a pragmatic and realistically feasible way (meta goal)

(P5) Finally, the feasibility aspect shall constantly be kept in mind by conducting a **reality check** with each chosen methodology. This means for each selected methodology the question will be raised: can this methodology realistically be applied within the given frame ("how" dimension)?

With this set of key requirements in mind, the following sections will explain the chosen methodologies one after another. Simultaneously, a short reasoning for the selection of each will be given, also taking up the above key design principles.

2.3.2 Case Study

"Science drives practice which drives science" (Latham, 2001, S. 1). At large, this entire research project aims at creating novel insights not for an end in itself, but to deduce valuable findings which can be translated into business practice, to actually generate added value. In consequence, discussed theories will be mirrored against the real-world example of Quemey in form of a case study, acting as overarching frame in which all other methodologies will be embedded later on.

Looking at the last hundred years, there was a lively **debate** whether the case study methodology can be accepted as proper scientific method or whether it is driven more by chance than logic (Yin, 1994, S. 283-284). In this light, Voss qualifies the role of the case methodology in research as a paradox, characterized by frequent application in business research on one side of the medal, but also by strong resistance towards the case study approach in certain communities on the other hand, almost reducing case studies to exploratory research. Accordingly, there are conceptual dissimilarities regarding a common understanding of what a case study represents – or precisely, whether it is about theory-building, testing, practice or theory (Voss, 2008, S. XVII). Dul and Hak address this problem by formulating a definition for the case study methodology which captures the main strands of existing elaborations: *"A case study is a study in which (a) one case (single case study) or a small number of cases (comparative case study) in their real life context are selected, and (b) scores obtained from* *these cases are analyzed in a qualitative manner"* (Dul & Hak, 2008, S. 4). This suggests differentiating between single case studies, in which data from only one instance are treated, and comparative case studies, where data from two or more instances are necessary to come to a solution (Dul & Hak, 2008, S. 4).

As compiled by Jans and Dittrich, case studies are particularly present in finance, strategy and HR management when assessing the number of respective publications, but also in operations and marketing, even though less often (Jans & Dittrich, 2008, S. 21). Moreover, their analysis of existing literature allowed them to draw the conclusion that the case study approach is a helpful research methodology for three **main areas** (Jans & Dittrich, 2008, S. 24): for broad and highly complex topics, for cases in which there is a little amount of theory available, and for topics in which the contextual situation is of special relevance.

Depending on author and concrete application context, there are **different guidelines** available on which steps should be performed when doing a case study. Resulting from this, there is a broad range of decision parameters to be specified when preparing a certain case study, and each of these decisions on parameters is further linked to methodological implications, which should be considered thoroughly (Meyer, 2001, S. 349). Meyer for example suggests a three-steps approach starting with the selection of relevant cases, followed by the sampling time, and finally the selection of data collection procedures. In each of these steps she offers a range of decision options (Meyer, 2001, S. 350). Other than that, Vissak recommends nine steps in order to get to high-quality case study papers. These steps comprise preparation activities like the identification of a research purpose and overall scope, the justification of the application of the case study approach, and a certain context description. It then succeeds the methodology part, with an explanation of case and respondents' selection as well as the decision on developing new theories or testing existing ones. Afterwards, the case itself is illustrated (with quotes or exemplary figures) and it is compared with relevant literature to derive conclusions. Finally, a summary completes the case study with a short wrap up of the gained findings and suggestions on their implications (Vissak, 2010, S. 383).

A case study is considered an **appropriate methodology** here, as its objectives and the portrayed application areas demonstrate its suitability for the underlying research question. This addresses precisely what P1 requires. Moreover, a case study can be designed uncomplicatedly, it is easily understandable, open for flexible adaptation and can be configured in a way that fits to Quemey, to the effect that P2-P5 are complied, too. The presented recommendations will be handled in the way that the nine-step process by Vissak will be consulted as basic course, though it will be loosely interpreted to meet Quemey's case. The discussed point of criticism that case studies are driven by chance rather than logic shall be encountered by using the case study approach as framework only, in which other scientific methods will be embedded systematically.

2.3.3 Business Modelling Frameworks

Ground-breaking innovations seldom stem from new products or technologies on their own. Instead, the overall BM is what makes the difference, with the interplay of products, applied technologies, processes, market entry strategies, and customer value being a decisive factor for success or failure (Gassmann, Frankenberger, & Csik, 2013, S. 4) (Ematinger, 2018, S. 15). According to Christensen, successful companies of the present are most likely to fail in the future: when sticking to their BM without critical reflection, the same processes which led to great success in the past will probably reject disruptive technologies in the future (Christensen C. M., 1997, S. 98). Hence, companies are permanently tasked with the renewal of their BM to cope with the changes in their environment (Ematinger, 2018, S. 21). Since this project aims at identifying a future-oriented BM for the startup Quemey, it is important to treat the scientific foundations of business modelling. In comparison to the other methodologies, this part will receive special attention, as the chosen BM framework is essential for developing a future-oriented BM for Quemey later on.

As constituted in the definitions section, a BM is understood as the fundamental logic that determines how a business works. To design such a logic, it is necessary to first understand its components. Earlier it became obvious that many authors have different perceptions on which key ingredients need to be part of a BM. In the following, different business modelling approaches will be explained and the most suitable for the present case will be selected.

One of the most well-known and most popular formats is the **business model canvas** (BMC) by Osterwalder and Pigneur. It is compiled by nine elementary building blocks, categorizable into the four main areas of most important customers, tangible value of the offering, necessary infrastructure and financial viability (Ematinger, 2018, S. 21-22). In its origin, it was created to describe, evaluate, visualize and adapt BMs (Osterwalder & Pigneur, Business Model Generation: A Handbook for Visionaries, Game Changers, and Challengers, 2010, S. 12), preferably in joint and agile group discussions (Osterwalder & Pigneur, Business Model Generation: A Handbook for Visionaries, Game Changers, and Challengers, 2010, S. 42). With their BMC as starting point, Osterwalder and Pigneur also created the value proposition canvas, highlighting the importance of a strong customer value proposition (Osterwalder A. , Pigneur, Bernarda, & Smith, 2014, S. 61). Furthermore, they published a personal branding canvas in "Business Model You" as one-pager with a distinct selection of building blocks to reinvent one's professional career (Clark, Osterwalder, & Pigneur, 2012, S. 57).

In the context of the Lean Startup movement, Ash Maurya helped the BMC approach to become even more prevalent (Ismail, Malone, & Van Geest, 2014, S. 130). As he writes in "Running Lean", his **lean canvas** (LC) further refined the original BMC, resulting in a helpful format to brainstorm on realistic BM options, to determine where to start, and to assure constant learning (Maurya, Running Lean. Iterate from Plan A to a Plan That Works, 2012, S. 23). The LC reduces the BMC to its core, which makes it even easier applicable and more pragmatic, whilst reducing its complexity. Moreover, it highlights the importance of orienting all activities towards the customer's key problem and solution, to the effect that Maurya explicitly anchored these two aspects in his LC.

Focusing on the specific characteristics of technical contexts, Hoffmeister developed a **framework for digital BMs**. Altogether, he compares digital BMs to machines: they are automat systems of hard- and software combinations which perform predetermined processes autonomously by using software agents, transforming certain inputs into outputs (Hoffmeister, 2015, S. 68-69). In contrast to conventional (analogue) BMs, machines solve problems in a standardized and formal manner, which causes high scalability. Thus, a machine developer solves a distinct problem not just once, but for all those who have this problem (Hoffmeister, 2015, S. 65). As a conclusion, Hoffmeister summarizes that digital BMs consist of three different control loops: input, processing, and output (Hoffmeister, 2015, S. 78-79), which account for the three main pillars of the respective technology architecture (input clients, application server, output clients) (Hoffmeister, 2015, S. 110). Between these pillars, there are up- and down-transactions performed. Finally, the described construct is doubled, for each of the two sides in an exchange relationship, and the technological architecture is enhanced by the described triad of input, processing, and output (Hoffmeister, 2015, S. 112-117).

Narrowing down the topic area even further, Walter created a **reference model for platform businesses**. Because more and more technology companies (particularly software houses) grow into powerful market positions today, he draws the conclusion that it is usually not due to their technology, but because they know how to wrap technological innovations into disruptive (platform) BMs. According to Walter's findings, 13 out of 15 internet companies run a platform BM (Walter M. , Plattform-Geschäftsmodelle verstehen und entwickeln, 2017, S. 5-10). In this context, platforms are defined as businesses that operate either virtual or physical places, allowing two (or more) groups to identify, jointly create and exchange value (Walter M. , Plattform-Geschäftsmodelle verstehen und entwickeln, 2017, S. 13). This being said, it makes sense to differentiate between consumers, producers, partners and platform operators with the following key functions (Walter M. , Plattform-Geschäftsmodelle verstehen und entwickeln, 2017, S. 14), each equipped with a tangible flea market comparison supporting their understanding:[4]

- **Consumers** use the exchanged values or platform goods and can even be prosumers, when developing values on their own (e.g. flea market visitors).
- **Producers** provide values or platform goods via the platform infrastructure (e.g. flea market stallholders).
- **Partners** offer additional services, but are linked to the platform's values or goods only indirectly (e.g. flea market hot dog or refreshment stand).
- **Platform operators** run the platform and develop the vision behind it. They are responsible for core processes, marketing and sales, as well as constant review and development (e.g. flea market organizer).

Classical (physical) BMs depict linear businesses, characterized by value provisioning through product or service usage itself, where individual demand is independent from other market participants' demand. On the contrary, platform businesses provide value by the fact that third parties use the platform as well. Hence, the demand of one side depends on the other side's demand, and the platform plays the role of a central orchestrator, as it supplies the network and runs the respective infrastructure (Walter M. , Plattform-Geschäftsmodelle verstehen und entwickeln, 2017, S. 15) (Clement & Schreiber, 2016, S. 267). This setting enables network effects as mentioned before: users profit from the number of other platform users, both directly and indirectly, as e.g. more users can be equated with more interaction possibilities (Walter M. , Plattform-Geschäftsmodelle verstehen und entwickeln, 2017, S. 16) (Clement & Schreiber, 2016, S. 267). At the same time, this is what drives the chicken-and-egg problem: the overall attractiveness of the platform is determined by the balance between participants on the market sides, as more participants lead to more assumed interaction possibilities and thus higher value expectation (Walter M. , Plattform-Geschäftsmodelle verstehen und entwickeln, 2017, S. 17) (Clement & Schreiber, 2016, S. 281). Accordingly, the plain exchange of

---

[4] The flea market comparison was presented by Matthias Walter in a live webinar (08.12.2017).

goods for money is replaced by new monetization strategies for platform businesses, such as making money from transaction fees (like eBay), reach (like Youtube), access fees (like XING) or premium services whilst a basic version is offered for free (like Vimeo) (Walter M. , Plattform-Geschäftsmodelle verstehen und entwickeln, 2017, S. 18). The latter is titled freemium model, but in contrast to what the name suggests, freemium does not necessarily mean "for free" – it implies a certain form of reciprocity. The returns are oftentimes goods of strategic relevance in the internet, such as attention, faster distribution or reputation (Clement & Schreiber, 2016, S. 189-190).

In order to exploit their full potential and actually realize the maximum possible customer value, platform businesses need to pay attention to the special characteristics of platform models, and anchor them in their BM. They need to move on from classical linear BMs towards platform-appropriate ones (Walter M. , Plattform-Geschäftsmodelle verstehen und entwickeln, 2017, S. 21). Walter addresses this ambition with his platform innovation kit, containing a five-stages toolset that supports a systematical platform BM definition. For each of these stages, there is a respective canvas suggested, as compiled below.

Table 1: Platform Business Model Development Steps

No.	Step 1	Step 2	Step 3	Step 4	Step 5
Title	Environment Scan	Ideation	Value Proposition	Service Design	Strategy Definition
Goal	Analyse influence factors from the surrounding: -Key trends -Market forces -Industry forces -Macroeconomics	Create first draft of platform business depiction, incl.: -Value proposition, value stream(s) and revenue model -for peers, consumers, producers and partners	Capture central value creation mechanisms of the platform, incl.: -Core/ mission, transactions and value propositions -For consumers, producer, partners and platform owner	Define central design parameters of core platform services for consumers, producers and partners, incl.: -Activities -Resources -Technology	Compile overarching platform strategy based on -Influencers like stakeholders, business drivers and competitors -Positioning regarding vision, USP, unfair advantage and mission -Strategies for resource,

Tool	Platform Environment Canvas	Platform Idea Canvas	Platform Value Canvas	Platform Service Canvas	business case and market
					Platform Strategy Canvas

Source: own representation of the author based on (Walter, Lohse, & Guzman, Platform Innovation Kit, 2017, S. 9)

The core is depicted by the platform value canvas (PVC) in step 3, being a four-layered circle that assesses participants, mission, value propositions and transactions (incl. money flows). Each aspect is to be evaluated for each platform participant role separately (consumers, producers, partners, platform operators), to do justice to the platform property of multidimensionality (Walter M. , Plattform-Geschäftsmodelle verstehen und entwickeln, 2017, S. 24).

This description now allows for a comparison of the models' main characteristics. Altogether, this provides a sound basis to select which framework shall be applied later. To assure a systematic selection procedure and to reduce subjectivity to a minimum, a **scoring model** shall help to rate each presented framework. This rating will consider the key design principles from chapter 2.3.1, to assess each framework candidate against what is important for the present project. In tangible terms: a ten-stage rating scale will be applied, with 1 representing a very low level of fulfilment regarding the respective design principle, and with 10 being the maximum level possible. By adding up all points per framework, a rank order can be deduced, which reveals the framework that fits the present context best (see Table 2). One might argue that the distributed points for each framework might still underlie a certain subjectivity, but for this reason, each scoring will be equipped with a reasoning along the key design principles criteria:

P1 (leads to relevant insights): As the PVC appears to be the model that is most precisely tailored to a technology-based platform business like Quemey, this framework receives 10 points. In relation to this rating, the Digital BM addresses at least the particularities of digital businesses, allowing a rating of 7 points. Instead, the two canvas models are both generalist models, hence they have less topic-specific relevance, even though the LC is at least often applied in agile development. Therefore, it receives 6 points, whilst the BMC gets 5 points.

P2 (not overwhelmingly complex): In this dimension, any rating depends on the definition of complexity. For the purpose of pragmatism, its definition is in this case narrowed down to the number of elements that each framework contains. From this perspective, the PVC with only four main areas appears to be the least complex framework, although these four points are to be assessed for each of the four distinguished participant roles. This allows for an 8-points scoring. Next, as its name and the underlying philosophy suggests, the LC is ought to be a lean, uncomplex tool. Notwithstanding, it consists of nine different fields that need to be completed, which explains the rating of 7 points. The BMC is compiled by nine fields as well, but within these there is oftentimes more detail required, leading to 6 points. Hoffmeister's Digital BM asks for twelve questions (see **Error! Reference source not found.**), being the most complex alternative, and is thus rated with 4 points.

P3 (easily understandable): As outlined for the aspect of complexity, the LC is designed as a streamlined version of the BMC. Maurya himself describes it as fast, concise and portable instrument (Maurya, Running Lean. Iterate from Plan A to a Plan That Works, 2012, S. 5-6). Nonetheless, a few background information on the Lean Startup approach are needed to fully understand its nature, but apart from that it can be applied easily and quickly – e.g. in a 15 minutes brainstorming for version 1.0, which can then be tested with other people (Maurya, Running Lean. Iterate from Plan A to a Plan That Works, 2012, S. 26). The same counts for the BMC, which is (with certain backgrounds) easily applicable, too. Hence, the LC is rated with 8 points, the BMC with 7 points. Walter's PVC is easily understandable when being familiar with platform economics, and partly because of its uncomplex structure with four major components only, leading to 6 points. Finally, Hoffmeister's framework requires huge background knowledge in terms of digital businesses and even technology and software foundations, which justifies 3 points.

P4 (flexible for adaptation): Generally speaking, each model can be modified if the user wishes to do so. On the other hand, none of the frameworks comes with fields in blank which are explicitly intended to leave room for further suggestions or relevant aspects to find influence. For the fact that the BMC proved its adaptability already, as the LC is designed from it, both canvas models receive 6 points, whereas the other two frameworks get 5 points each.

P5 (reality check): Having in mind the overarching meta goal of pragmatism and feasibility, it is an important question which of the discussed tools is most probably applied in the real world – here for Quemey. Mainly because of its outstanding topic relevance, the PVC was introduced to one of Quemey's founders. His reaction expressed that he could imagine using this framework for Quemey, as he judged the framework very appropriate. Additionally, he noted that it is crucial to precisely define the included roles, since different participants could own multiple roles depending on the respective situations (Schütz, Interview: Quemey, 2017, S. 1). This statement depicts a solid basis for a 10-points rating. Other than that, both canvases are oftentimes applied in business practice (Ematinger, 2018, S. 21) (Ismail, Malone, & Van Geest, 2014, S. 130), which verifies their practicability and hence 8 points each. Contrarily, the Digital BM shows implementation barriers, resulting from the required technological knowledge (see above). Thus, 4 points seem appropriate here.

This being sad, the rating is completed, as visualized in Table 2. Looking at the total sum per suggested framework, it appears to be Walter's Platform BM that suits the context of the present topic best. Thus, it will be chosen as framework to assess and develop Quemey's current and future BMs in the third chapter.

Table 2: Selection of Business Modelling Framework

	BMC (Osterwalder/ Pigneur)	LC (Maurya)	Digital BM (Hoffmeister)	Platform BM (Walter)
P1: leads to relevant insights	5	6	7	10
P2: not overwhelmingly complex	6	7	4	8
P3: easily understandable	7	8	3	6
P4: flexible for adaptation	6	6	5	5

P5: reality check	8	8	4	10
Total sum	**32**	**35**	**23**	**39**

Source: own representation of the author based on described findings from literature (see above)

2.3.4 Customer Interviews

Whenever introducing new products or services, it is commonly considered a crucial initial step to validate one's innovation by collecting actual customer feedback. This holds true for both the Lean Startup approach as mentioned in the introduction (Ries, 2011, S. 5), and for classical market research as taught in marketing theory (Bode, 2014, S. 25-26). *"Startups often accidently build something nobody wants, it does not matter much if they do it on time and on budget. The goal of a startup is to figure out the right thing to build – the thing customers want and will pay for (...)"* (Ries, 2011, S. 20). In line with this philosophy, Quemey's current BM shall later be validated with potential users. To learn as much as possible about potential user's opinions within a minimum amount of time and effort, a **two steps data collection process** was chosen to generate customer feedback, which will be outlined theoretically and methodologically now.

"The fastest way to learn is to talk to customers" (Maurya, Running Lean. Iterate from Plan A to a Plan That Works, 2012, S. 71). And wherever there is a more profound understanding of the behaviour of market participants desired, the methodology of **qualitative (customer) interviews** comes into play (Aghamanoukjan, Buber, & Michael, 2009, S. 420). Based on the findings obtained from these interviews, first assumptions on the research object can be derived (in this case first indications on general user acceptance and Quemey's current product design). In step two, the interview findings are to be validated in a more quantitative approach with a larger panel. This approach to use a first qualitative investigation and to double check the conclusions with a subsequent quantitative study has been recommended and applied successfully in many research projects yet (Bode, 2014, S. 51) (Heitger & Serfass, 2015, S. 399).

As far as the interview preparation is concerned, literature typically suggests creating an **interview guideline** (Maurya, Running Lean. Iterate from Plan A to a Plan That Works, 2012, S. 74). It has the function to assure that all interviews are focusing on the most relevant, central questions, whilst at the same time it shall open up flexibility for topics that have not been considered in advance (Bode, 2014, S. 51). In the present case, Ash Maurya's problem and solution interview design is chosen as starting point.

The **problem interview** aims at validating the problem section in Maurya's LC (see chapter 2.3.3). More precisely: it shall test whether one's own proposal of the customers' key problems actually depicts what matters most to them. Having assured that this is the case, the next step is to come up with a solution that helps customers to solve their most relevant issues. This task is done by conducting **solution interviews**, testing a first demo of the developed solution with potential customers. As Maurya poses, it is important to have a realizable, realistically looking, quick to iterate and minimum waste demo version of one's product, ideally in form of a mock-up (Maurya, Running Lean. Iterate from Plan A to a Plan That Works, 2012, S. 95-97). At this stage, also pricing should come into play, to test whether the solution actually provides value to customers which they are willing to pay for (Maurya, Running Lean. Iterate from Plan A to a Plan That Works, 2012, S. 98).

In addition to those aspects relating to interview guidelines, Maurya suggests certain **interview clues** for good results. To his mind, interviews should be conducted in 1:1 situations rather than with focus groups, to avoid group think. Further, he outlines the advantageousness of face to face interview situations as this enables to see body language (Maurya, Running Lean. Iterate from Plan A to a Plan That Works, 2012, S. 71-72), and of pursuing an open and flexible interview style, allowing for versatile adaptations of the prepared interview guideline. Moreover, Maurya states that the interview content should be wrapped in a frame, to impede the impression of pitching, and that one should rather observe what customers do instead of asking them what they want (Maurya, Running Lean. Iterate from Plan A to a Plan That Works, 2012, S. 73-74). Additionally, he recommends addressing a huge, unspecified target group, which is not narrowed down too far already, *"to avoid running into a local-maxima problem"* (Maurya, Running Lean. Iterate from Plan A to a Plan That Works, 2012, S. 74). Ultimately, Maurya advises to conduct interviews in company, to ask for enough time, to avoid incentives for participation, to record the interview partners, to assure instant documentation of the interview results, and ultimately to interview 30-60 people for valuable learnings (Maurya, Running Lean. Iterate from Plan A to a Plan That Works, 2012, S. 75-76). All these hints shall be kept in mind when designing an interview setting for the present research project later on.

After all, this interview approach is to be checked for **compliance of the key design principles** as stated in chapter 2.3.1. As the suggested interview guideline will be designed in accordance with the overall research question, P1 can be confirmed, since it is obvious that questions will only be added if they can actually contribute to the pursued research topic. Moreover, as the foundation for these interviews comes from Maurya's Lean Startup approach, P2 and P3 are fulfilled, too. Lean by definition stands for the elimination of waste (Maurya, Running Lean. Iterate from Plan A to a Plan That Works, 2012, S. XXIII) – consequently, both uncomplex products and simple, but early solutions are key components. Next, the confirmation of P4 is dependent on the actual handling of Maurya's problem and solution interview guidelines when developing and adapting one for the present topic. Quemey's interview guideline is to be designed with maximum flexibility, and also the conduct of the interviews themselves is designed with the intention of allowing alternative conversation lines when appearing appropriate in the individual situations. In addition, the interview guideline can be further modified after the first couple of interviews are conducted, to further increase its accuracy (Bode, 2014, S. 51). Finally, interviews are frequently performed nowadays, as many examples from every day's life come to mind when thinking about one's own interview experiences. Thus, also interviews for Quemey can easily be imagined, and P5 is assured, too.

2.3.5 Customer Survey

Having gained first findings from these interviews, a verification with a larger panel shall be conducted. Whilst interviews are designed as rather open data collection method – it cannot be foreseen what customers will answer or say – an online survey in step two will help to further substantiate the interview learnings. Generally speaking, this leads to rather quantitative results, as standardized data collected from a larger panel can be evaluated and summarized in statistics, in contrast to rather qualitative statements from interviews.

In market research literature, qualitative and quantitative approaches are oftentimes presented as the exact opposite of each other. Nonetheless, the targeted and systematic combination of both can be appropriate for the profound and overarching answering of certain research questions. As a result, the so-called **Mixed Methods** emerged. Meanwhile, they have established as serious alternative to quantitative and qualitative research in the scientific discussion, particularly in the Anglo-American region (Foscht, Angerer, & Swoboda, 2009, S. 249). The chosen approach for the present case can be termed a Mixed Methods approach. As such, it depicts an empiric research project, following a typical **research process design**. Foscht et al. characterize the stereotypical research process in a three-step model (Foscht, Angerer, & Swoboda, 2009, S. 250):

1. Conception phase: definition of research question
2. Empirical phase: data collection and data evaluation
3. Conclusion phase: deduction of key findings

Both the interview and the survey which shall validate Quemey's solution with potential customers belong to the empirical phase. Here, Decker and Wagner differentiate between primary and secondary research, with primary research being defined as collection of own data, e.g. via surveys, interviews or observation, and with secondary research meaning the evaluation of data that do exist already (Foscht, Angerer, & Swoboda, 2009, S. 249-250) (Decker & Wagner, 2002, S. 21). The present case depicts a multi-pronged primary research approach, characterized by applying multiple methods on the same question (Foscht, Angerer, & Swoboda, 2009, S. 251).

Looking at the second component of the chosen Mixed Methods design, the planned **survey** can be understood as classical data collection method for empirically oriented disciplines in social or economic sciences. Even though surveys went through an extensive evolution in the past decades – according to Reinecke, Scheuch's definition of surveys being a special type of interviews still holds true (Reinecke, 2014, S. 601): as research instruments, interviews are understood as systematic processes with scientific objectives, in which the test subject is caused to provide verbal information by targeted questions or communicated stimuli (Scheuch, 1973, S. 70). Consequently, a survey is the result of a questioned person's reaction in a communication process (Reinecke, 2014, S. 601).

Surveys can be differentiated according to their **degree of standardization** in terms of their question texts, answer categories and the order of questions. A higher level of standardization assures that different answers actually stem from different declarations. Whilst qualitative research designs, such as guided interviews, usually rely on survey techniques with a lower degree of standardization, quantitative social sciences pursue a higher one (Reinecke, 2014, S. 601). One of the main goals of standardization is to enable the direct comparison of research objects, with random sampling, questionnaire and the interaction between interviewers and interviewees designed to assure objectivity and harmonization of results (Reinecke, 2014, S. 603).

A key element of each survey is represented by the **questionnaire**. In market research literature, there are many recommendations for its design, e.g. distinguishing between different types of questions relating to the desired insights or different scale designs (Reinecke, 2014, S. 604-608). As the intention for the present project is to use the survey to validate the interview findings, the survey questionnaire will be derived from the interview guideline. Thus, question types and questionnaire design will not be discussed extensively at this point.

Regarding the **channel** via which a survey is run, online surveys use the internet as communication medium (Wagner & Hering, 2014, S. 661). In order to determine the methodology of an online survey as appropriate for a distinct research question, both advantages and disadvantages of this survey type are to be considered. Due to the applied medium, online surveys are location- and time-independent. Hence, there are more possibilities to reach participants in an easy and low-cost way (Heitger & Serfass, 2015, S. 399), as the internet connects the entire world. Moreover, graphical visualizations can make the survey more convenient for the participant, and even multimedia content can be integrated. Moreover, interviewer effects are impeded, which may result in less socially desirable response patterns. Additionally, data recording is happening automatically, not manually, and surveys can be realized with low financial effort as there are plenty of free online survey tools available. On the other side, reaching the desired target audience is usually more difficult than with other survey types. It is questionable whether the target audience can actually be caught via the pursued communication and survey promotion channels (Wagner & Hering, 2014, S. 662-663). This shall be kept in mind when turning these recommendations into practice later on.

Again, the postulated **key design principles** are to be checked for fulfilment. Like it was the case for the customer interviews, the survey questions are to be derived from the overarching research question, to the effect that P1 is confirmed. Further, as recommended in the relevant literature as well, the survey design may not be overwhelmingly complex, and it should be as comfortable as possible for all participants, which implies it should be easily understandable. Hence, P2 and P3 are complied, too. Besides, the survey design can be modified flexibly, since the suggestions from literature are understood as starting point only, not as something set in stone. Finally, the ubiquity of online survey tools (many even for free) encourages a low-effort realization, thus also the last two remaining design principles are assured.

Comparing the Lean Startup perspective from chapter 2.3.4 and the Mixed Methods approach in the light of classical market research, it becomes obvious that they are designed with two different mind-sets. Notwithstanding, the seemingly different approaches do not contradict each other. It is rather the case that both discuss the same elementary content, but wrapped in different taxonomies and terminologies, depending on the respective angle. On one hand, the Lean Startup approach puts special emphasis on engaging customers during the entire product development process, in order to test a vision by talking to customers and measuring how customers behave, and thereby learning as much as possible with a minimum waste of resources (Maurya, Running Lean. Iterate from Plan A to a Plan That Works, 2012, S. XXII). On the other hand, classical market research theory focuses on the scientific research process as frame of reference for each empirical study (Foscht, Angerer, & Swoboda, 2009, S. 249). Thus, the latter angle is characterized rather by academic intentions than by economic interests. Nonetheless, both perspectives aim at explaining or verifying an observed phenomenon. Hence, these two views shall be combined here, to generate optimal findings by merging the best of both worlds.

2.3.6 Scenario Analysis

Whilst the sketched interview and survey approach is ought to validate Quemey's current problem and solution design, the overarching research question focuses on a second part, too: it also aims at developing a future-oriented next level BM for Quemey, which by definition implies a certain occupation with the future. In order to structure this "forecasting" process according to scientific requirements, the **methodology of scenario thinking** shall be applied.

"The global financial crisis and its aftermath are clear evidence of what can happen when the future is seen as a continuation of a seemingly rosy present" (Wright & Cairns, 2011, S. 3). To cope with this problem, scenario thinking has proven as helpful tool for thinking about what could happen in the future, as it creates a rough frame of the expectable by developing best- and worst-case scenarios. Moreover, the emotional comprehension of what could happen is made easier thereby (Heitger & Serfass, 2015, S.

401). Understanding possible alternatives in advance improves a company's capacity for action, since it is prepared for decisions beforehand. Besides, thinking about different cases reduces complexity, since irrelevant ones can be suppressed (Kerth, Asum, & Stich, 2015, S. 230).

Both threats and opportunities are considered, as well as multiple influence factors from political, legal, or market-related developments, to list a few examples (Kerth, Asum, & Stich, 2015, S. 230) (Wright & Cairns, 2011, S. 1). Hence, the consequences of changes in all considered external and internal influence factor dimensions are systematically played through. This serves to recognize trends, reduce uncertainty and prepare economic actions. Altogether, the gained estimates about the future feed into a company's strategic planning, characterizing a scenario analysis as strategic instrument (Kerth, Asum, & Stich, 2015, S. 231).

On the other hand, **critics** query the subjectivity inherent in the methodology, requesting a more science-based approach when management and organization topics are concerned. This includes the understanding of strategy activities as rational process that should be free from subjective influences. Reacting to this standpoint, Wright and Cairns state that scenario thinking may be an art discipline to a certain extent, but nonetheless management and organization considerations can by their nature not be devoid of subjectivity. Moreover, scenario thinking takes objective factors into account – but a distinct degree of subjectivity remains, with personal beliefs influencing the scenario development and rating. Thus, science and art join forces in this methodology (Wright & Cairns, 2011, S. 15-16).

Moving on to how the **process of scenario thinking** is typically conducted, there is no generally accepted and commonly applied approach existing. Instead, many different approaches and procedures are labelled as methods of scenario analysis. Looking at relevant literature, authors typically focus on one special approach, on partial aspects or on rating different approaches according to different criteria (Ulbrich Zürni, 2004, S. 13-14). As inferred by Susanne Ulbrich Zürni, scenario analysis is defined as flexible approach that offers different possibilities of scenario development. Further, it is open to integration or combination with other techniques. In line with this, the term "scenario" is understood as description of a future situation and its course of development leading to this situation (Ulbrich Zürni, 2004, S. 14).

Kerth et al. for example suggest a five-step **procedure** consisting of problem analysis (1), influence analysis (2), trend exploration (3), scenario development and interpretation (4), and finally evaluation (5). The expected outcome of this is a set of scenarios (best, worst and normal case) including disruptive events, risks and opportunities (Kerth, Asum, & Stich, 2015, S. 233-234). Alternatively, Kerth et al. outline a second approach as applied by Siemens, starting with the imagination of futuristic scenarios (Kerth, Asum, & Stich, 2015, S. 234-235). The latter is considered to be more subjective (even though refined by Siemens in the meantime (Siemens, no release date specified, S. 6)), as these future imaginations seem less systematically concluded, and more based on creativity or ingenuity.

In contrast, the Chair of Business Administration, Environmental Management and Accounting at Technische Universität Dresden has an even broader understanding of which elements are implied in the scenario analysis process. It goes beyond the pure analysis of scenarios, since it also encompasses the development of options for action, including the decision for one's preferred option and its implementation (Günther, no release date specified, S. 1). Against the background that this project aims at answering its research question in a pragmatic and realistically feasible way, this implementation-oriented approach is chosen as guideline when the later elaboration of scenarios in the case study part follows. As suggested by Günther, the following steps will be performed in a slightly adopted manner: goal determination (1), environment analysis (2), scenario creation (3), vision development (4), options for action (5), implementation (6) (Günther, no release date specified, S. 1).

According to Hinterhuber, the **number of developed scenarios** should not be limited to best- and worst-case scenarios, as suggested by the well-known scenario funnel image (Kerth, Asum, & Stich, 2015, S. 231), since they are not sufficient to describe complex and uncertain developments. Likewise, three scenarios tend to encourage the selection of the middle one. In consequence, Hinterhuber advises modelling four scenarios

(Hinterhuber, 2015, S. 121). Having defined these four and chosen one's preferred option, it is then necessary to determine a strategy road map, defining the aspired next steps (Hinterhuber, 2015, S. 123).

This being said, it is again necessary to check the scenario analysis methodology against the postulated **key design principles** from 2.3.1. Regarding P1 and the relevance for the overarching research question, scenario thinking particularly addresses the aspect of future orientation. Concerning P2 and P3, the methodology may neither be too complex nor too hard to understand. Both depends on how the tool is applied later on, meaning the level of detail that is reached in the scenario development for Quemey. As far as the instrument itself is concerned, it is neither considered too complex nor too hard to understand, since it depicts a commonly known strategy tool. Further – as explicitly shown above – scenario analysis is open to adaptation and enhancement, so that P4 is complied. Finally, there is nothing to be said against the practical application in the case of Quemey, which is why also P5 can be confirmed.

2.3.7 Expert Interviews

Ultimately, one last methodology remains: the following section provides a brief overview about **expert interviews**, serving as foundation for their later application to substantiate the drawn conclusions in the case study part with expert statements. As far as a classification into the landscape of empirical research is concerned, expert interviews are again a method of primary research, as they collect new data. Beyond that, they stem from qualitative social sciences – nonetheless, the degree of qualitativity is heavily determined by the level of standardization of the interview guideline. (Bogner, Littig, & Menz, 2014, S. 1-2).

A central goal of expert interviews is commonly considered to be the generation of information in a pragmatic, effective and efficient way. Provided that experts are condensation points of knowledge, simply asking them for the relevant questions can save huge amounts of money, time and effort for a researcher (Bogner, Littig, & Menz, 2014, S. 2). This supports Kaiser's definition of qualitative expert interviews: to his point of view, qualitative expert interviews depict a standardized, theory-led approach of data collection by surveying people who have exclusive knowledge in the topic of interest (Kaiser, 2014, S. 6). It is particularly suitable for case studies, since they typically seek to dive deep into a very specific topic, rather than capturing the maximum of possibilities (Kaiser, 2014, S. 4).

The research question is usually taken as starting point to determine which information are desired from an expert interview. Hence, the research question needs to be mirrored against the experiential world of the expert, for the researcher to derive appropriate **interview questions**, which then lead to relevant answers. These answers eventually allow conclusions on the initial research question. Generally, an interview **guideline** consolidates all posed questions, helping the researcher to steer and structure the interview situation (Kaiser, 2014, S. 4-5). But: treating it with a certain degree of flexibility helps to do justice to the individual interview's particularities, contributing to optimal results. In an analogous manner, the research question is to be consulted when determining who is considered a relevant **expert** (Mey & Mruck, 2010, S. 427). The selection of appropriate experts is typically named as one of the main critics, since the quality of results is heavily influenced by who is asked (Bogner, Littig, & Menz, 2014, S. 9). In its origin, the term "expert" descends from the Latin word "expertus", which can be translated with "tested" or "proved". Resulting from this, experts are normally understood as specialists or referees, so one could argue which factors characterize somebody as specialist in a certain area. Could not everybody be an expert in their special field? Transposed to research, Bogner et al. define experts as context-dependent concerning the treated research question and a social representativeness at the same time. This means an expert is classified as such by both the researcher in terms of the relevant research area, and by society regarding a matching function, reputation or the like (Bogner, Littig, & Menz, 2014, S. 11-12). Ensuring that both is complied counters the criticism of determining experts by subjective assessment.

For the expert interview evaluation, the methodology of **qualitative content analysis** shall be applied. The respective techniques have become a standard methodology in social sciences in the meantime, coming from the challenge to evaluate huge amounts of data material (Mayring, Qualitative Inhaltsanalyse, 2010, S. 601). This data material can come from open interview transcripts, expert interviews, focus groups, observation protocols of case studies, files, articles, internet material, promotion material or other documents (Mayring & Fenzl, Qualitative Inhaltsanalyse, 2014, S. 543) (Mayring & Brunner, Qualitative Inhaltsanalyse, 2009, S. 673). In detail, a qualitative content analysis transfers technical know-how regarding the handling of extensive text material to running an interpretative text analysis, whilst assuring intersubjective verifiability. Mayring lists three basic techniques for doing so (Mayring, Qualitative Inhaltsanalyse, 2010, S. 602):

- Summaries reduce texts to key messages (e.g. by inductive category creation)
- Explanations make texts more understandable by putting them into context
- Structuralizations underline important aspects through cross-evaluation (e.g. by deductive category building to systematize the respective material).

For each technique, the application of a specific **procedure model** is suggested (Mayring & Brunner, Qualitative Inhaltsanalyse, 2009, S. 674) (Mayring & Fenzl, Qualitative Inhaltsanalyse, 2014, S. 548). For the purpose of pragmatism, a simplified version of a rather abstract reference model will be used, combining deductive and inductive approaches as proposed by Mayring and Fenzl. This reference model starts with the clarification of the overall problem, followed by selecting and classifying the research material. Subsequently, after defining the analysis entities, the determination of categories and the respective abstraction level succeed, either inductive (bottom up) or deductive (top down) (Mayring & Fenzl, Qualitative Inhaltsanalyse, 2014, S. 548-550).

Concerning the operational performance of this procedure, there are **software** solutions available to support the researcher. They offer manifold possibilities of data organization, categorization, keyword search and the like – saving time and helping to handle huge amounts of data. On the other side, software runs processes that are technically feasible, without assuring that all relevant content-wise aspects are considered (Bogner, Littig, & Menz, 2014, S. 83-84). For this reason, the present project will not rely on software support, since the scientific evaluation process is in the foreground, rather than plain results.

As the discussed characteristics and application instructions shall serve as directive for the present project, it is one more time necessary to compare the expert interview methodology with the **postulated key design principles**. Regarding the methodology's significance for the research question, the above illustration outlined that expert interviews are genuinely oriented towards an underlying research question. Further, as mentioned before they depict a pragmatic and thus easily understandable instrument, whose complexity can be held down by designing an uncomplicated guideline, resulting in P2 and P3 being complied. Lastly, the flexible handling of the interview plan was recommended above, so that P4 is met, and it can easily be imagined identifying and interviewing relevant experts from one's own (business) environment, leading to a fulfilled fifth design principle. On that account, expert interviews are estimated a fruitful amendment to the other methodologies in the present research design.

Having described all chosen methodologies, the following visualization (Figure 3) of the **overarching research design** illustrates which methodology supports which part of the knowledge production process in the later case study. As becomes obvious, this project does not focus on one single methodology, since a multi-method design was chosen. Each applied instrument was added for a distinct delimited aspect, contributing to its individual part of the holistic big picture.

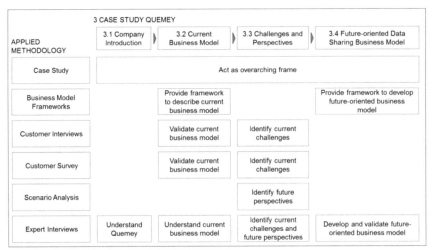

Figure 3: Overarching Research Design
Source: own representation of the author; blue boxes mark the individual role or contribution
of each applied methodology (green boxes on the left) for the respective case study parts
(green boxes on top)

3 Practical Examination: Case Study Quemey

3.1 Company Introduction

3.1.1 Overview

Now that the overarching research design with all comprised methodologies was explained, its practical application can follow in the subsequent case study part. In total, this aims at mirroring the findings from literature against the real-world example of the startup Quemey, to develop a future-oriented data sharing BM that helps Quemey to realize their vision with sustainable business success.

For this reason, the case study is **structured** as follows: after a brief overview about the company, their current BM will be elaborated. Further, it will be validated in terms of user acceptance (would people use Quemey's service) and core product design variables (which rewards would they prefer) by conducting customer interviews and a customer survey. Based on these findings, current challenges can be derived, and matched with future perspectives resulting from a scenario analysis. Finally, both the identified challenges and future perspectives will be taken up in the development of a future-oriented BM. During the entire process, expert interviews will augment the drawn conclusions with hypotheses from experts of digitalization, data-based BMs and startups as well as travelling, transport and logistics topics. Besides, statements of Quemey's founders and company-internal documents provide further valuable sources of information.

Officially founded in 2016, Quemey pursues the **vision** of enabling passengers on board of aircrafts to make better use of their most valuable resource: their time (Schütz & Fleischer, Quemey GmbH. Introduction Emirates, 2017, S. 2). This is enabled by their solution – the first worldwide – which provides aircraft passengers with a platform to answer surveys in exchange for incentives (Quemey, no release date specified, S. 2-3). An exemplary survey journey serves for illustration: on board the airplane, passengers select the WiFi portal and enter the provided survey via their

© Springer Fachmedien Wiesbaden GmbH, part of Springer Nature 2018
A. Dreller, *Creating Value from Data Sharing*, Informationsmanagement
in Theorie und Praxis, https://doi.org/10.1007/978-3-658-23276-4_3

smartphone, laptop or tablet. They complete the survey and thereby provide the airline (or a third party or market research company who commissioned e.g. a market research survey) with their data. In turn, air passengers receive an immediate reward, such as free inflight WiFi (Schütz & Fleischer, APEX 2017 LONG BEACH. Pitch Deck for Panasonic Avionics, 2017, S. 6). Quemey thereby addresses the needs of multiple stakeholders, like air passengers, airlines, avionic partners and market research companies (Quemey, no release date specified, S. 4-5).

To actually reach and explore the worlds of all stakeholders, Quemey pursues a **strategic partnership approach**. As will be outlined in their history later on, they signed partnership contracts with e.g. DTAG and GfK (Schütz & Fleischer, APEX 2017 LONG BEACH. Pitch Deck for Panasonic Avionics, 2017, S. 1). Moreover, they realized first PoCs with Virgin Atlantic and are currently in talks with other airlines to expand their network (Fleischer, 2017).

The **team** behind Quemey consists of the two founders Bastian Schütz and Dennis Fleischer, and a team of external (software) developers. Additionally, Quemey is supported by their advisory board, compiled by representatives of LinkedIn, different DTAG subsidiaries and GfK (Schütz & Fleischer, Quemey Company Profile, 2017, S. 2). Later on, the section on Quemey's history and vision will take a closer look at the team, particularly regarding the story of its formation. But first of all, the following chapter will point out Quemey's key problems and solutions in the light of Ash Maurya's Running Lean philosophy.

3.1.2 Key Problems and Solutions

Even though this aspect is a central part of a company's BM, and will thus be treated in 3.2 again, it is considered such a central element and starting point that it will now be sketched in brief. To understand what Quemey aspires to do, it is necessary to first analyze their key problems and solutions. As mentioned before, Quemey pursues a **multidimensional problem and solution approach**, focusing on problems of multiple stakeholder groups as shown in Table 3:

Table 3: Quemey's Key Problems and Solutions per Stakeholder Group

Stakeholder Group	Problem	Solution
Air passengers	...want to spend less time waiting and make better use of their flight time	Quemey offers interesting surveys that are rewarded with attractive incentives immediately
Airlines	...want to deliver excellent service and therefore need more information about customers	Quemey offers access to customer data and consulting services how to turn them into value
Avionic partners	...want to provide excellent inflight systems to enable best customer experience	Quemey offers an additional service component that can easily be integrated via open APIs (application programming interface)
Market research	...want to get information from an exclusive and "captured" target audience	Quemey offers the first ever access worldwide to air passengers during flights

Source: own representation of the author

In essence, Quemey's central instrument to provide all these solutions to the respective requestor is their **analytics platform**. It is accessible via the passengers' own devices – they simply need to log into the on-board WiFi – or via the aircraft's IFEC systems (inflight entertainment and connectivity systems). The platform supports all stages of a survey process, starting with managed survey development, and followed by its deployment. After passengers have completed the survey forms, the platform steers the reward provisioning process, and offers flexible and customized analytics and reporting services (Schütz & Fleischer, APEX 2017 LONG BEACH. Pitch Deck for Panasonic Avionics, 2017, S. 5).

On the other hand, the platform solution shall not be sold off-the-shelf forever. As "solution" suggests, it shall soon be accompanied by individual consulting services. Quemey seeks the dialogue with partners to meet their needs with recommended use cases. To get a closer look at the range of possibilities Quemey pitches, three **use cases** are pictured below (Schütz & Fleischer, APEX 2017 LONG BEACH. Pitch Deck for Panasonic Avionics, 2017, S. 10):

- Airlines could measure **real-time customer satisfaction** during the flight: passengers are sent a feedback survey, which they can access via the respective link on their own device that is connected to the on-board WiFi. The passengers express their current level of satisfaction, and Quemey's platform provides a real-time evaluation in tailored reports. Moreover, the cabin crew is given customer-specific suggestions how to react to the obtained feedback, to use the possibility of improving the passengers' flight experience.
- Airlines could collect **instant product and service feedback** from their passengers: after e.g. the on-board catering was distributed, passengers can rate their meal experience. Again, the purser receives a notification and can chose from a set of recommended reactions, to increase customer loyalty.
- Partners (e.g. market research companies) could run a classical market research survey to gain **customer insights**. As considered with e.g. LinkedIn, passengers use the WiFi portal to log into their LinkedIn account. They are asked to fill in a survey for a WiFi voucher, and LinkedIn would receive their data in turn.

But Quemey does not only seek the dialogue with corporate partners such as airlines or avionic partners: they also try to discover the world of the air passengers in more detail. One particularly important aspect is e.g. the question which kind of rewards is preferred by which customer group, and which kind of rewards is actually capable of motivating passengers to participate. This issue will be considered in chapter 3.2, when Quemey's current BM is described and validated by customer interviews and a subsequent survey. For now, Quemey's history and future vision shall follow, to round off their company profile.

3.1.3 History and Vision

The story of Quemey[5] can be traced back to a Deloitte innovation challenge in **2013**: together with a small team, Quemey's later founder Bastian Schütz participated in Deloitte's "Fasttrack Initiative Business Competition" in Sydney, which asked all participants to develop a $ 50mn business idea. In this context, Quemey's initial idea was born, as the team wanted to come up with something that enables people to make better use of flight time. They hypothesized that participating in surveys in exchange for incentives would delight air passengers. With this basic idea, Bastian's team won the Deloitte competition – but the idea remained an idea without subsequent actions.

Two years later, in **2015**, Bastian joined DTAG's trainee programme, in which he met Dennis Fleischer, the second founder of Quemey. By chance they came back to the idea of Quemey again, and they took it up as they believed in its potential. They quickly realized that they needed a broader perspective, not just the plain survey thought. As a result, they soon aimed at a multisided, overarching BM, also focusing on e.g. airlines or market research companies. If you will, this was the initial thought of a data sharing vision, which will be assessed in more depth later. Next, they began to think about the technical preconditions to bring surveys to air passengers. At this time, DTAG has just begun to launch WiFi inflight, so Bastian and Dennis started discussions with the DTAG WiFi experts, as the inflight WiFi portal seemed more feasible than integrating surveys into the on-board IFEC systems. To further validate and challenge their survey idea, Bastian and Dennis went to the Research and Results 2015 trade fair and pitched their idea to market research experts, questioning whether their idea has potential or is rather a pipe dream. They received extremely positive, affirmative feedback – but also scepticism whether they would actually manage to get surveys into airplanes, as this was considered a very challenging endeavour.

---

[5] The section on Quemey's history is based on the interviews with Quemey's founders. Additional information stem from (Schütz & Fleischer, Quemey GmbH. Introduction Emirates, 2017, p. 30).

All this happened in the first year after Bastian and Dennis had met and taken up the survey idea again. The more they worked on it, the more potential they saw– to the effect that they extended their talks to potential partners, aspiring to turn the support of e.g. DTAG into actual partnership contracts. Since the cooperation with DTAG required a GmbH foundation, Quemey was officially founded in mid **2016**. They also received financial support by DTAG in form of a huge investment, plus a three-months scholarship for the founders in the context of DTAG's corporate entrepreneurship programme UQBATE. Because of this, Bastian and Dennis were granted a period of three months off work, which they could fully dedicate to their idea. Over and above this, DTAG provided content-wise guidance in form of expert knowledge by DTAG representatives in Quemey's advisory board.

Another important milestone is depicted by the strategic cooperation with Virgin Atlantic. In mid 2016, Quemey conducted the first PoC with Virgin. This was merely driven by chance, because Virgin had an urgent need to realize a survey within one week preparation time only. 15.000 responses could be won – more than 50% of all passengers participated. At this point, Quemey had actual proof of user acceptance for the first time. One year later, Quemey and Virgin jointly started a second, larger pilot, which again showed satisfying participation levels.

Not only the technical realization or airline perspective are addressed with strategic cooperations – also the market research dimension of Quemey's BM. In mid **2017**, Quemey signed a partnership contract with GfK, embracing two joint pilots. These pilots also included data evaluation with GfK's existing customer data bases and tools. Moreover, GfK has many contacts to market research demanders, such as large cooperations wanting to align their products with customer needs.

In addition, the cooperation with DTAG caused another milestone in 2017: DTAG invited Quemey as corporate partner on the AIX aviation trade fair in Los Angeles, one of the largest trade fairs worldwide for airplane interior design.

Altogether, this leads to where Quemey is **right now**. They are trying to turn their survey BM into actual money in the short term, and they are trying to extend it towards a data sharing BM in the long run. This is Quemey's vision, since they seek for a data sharing approach, meaning they want to create user profiles which are enriched by further data attributes of other parties involved in the travelling value chain. Potential parties encompass e.g. transportation providers like Deutsche Bahn, airport parking facilities, airport shops, hotels at the passengers' target destinations and the like. The more data attributes that can be combined, the higher their expected value, as they are highly attractive for CRM cases like customer acquisition, increased loyalty or even retention by e.g. tailored offerings. This vision is to be taken up when developing Quemey's future-oriented BM later on. But when thinking about the future, it is helpful to start with analyzing the status quo, as the following section will do.

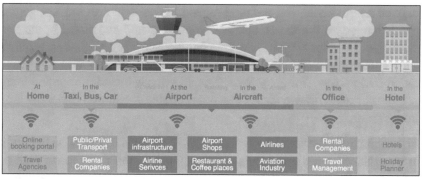

Figure 4: Quemey's Vision
Source: (Schütz & Fleischer, Quemey Company Profile, 2017, S. 10), provided by courtesy of Quemey 2018).

3.2 Current Business Model

3.2.1 Business Model Description

As the methodology section (2.3.3) could yield, Walter's platform business modelling approach shall serve to gather Quemey's current BM. Hence, the PVC as its centrepiece will be the focal point now. The recommended supporting procedure for its definition (Table 1), consisting of the five steps environment scan, ideation, value proposition, service design and strategy definition, will be applied only partly, mainly because not all steps fit to Quemey's context.

Starting with the **environment analysis**, Walter suggests evaluating key trends, market forces, industry forces and macroeconomic forces (Walter, Lohse, & Guzman, Platform Innovation Kit, 2017, S. 11), with market forces defined as customer and demand-related topics, and with industry forces characterized as the landscape of competitors and suppliers. At the first sight, this is – at least from a wording perspective – not mutually exclusive, since "market forces" could also imply other competitors in the respective market. Moreover, "industry forces" could equally include emerging technologies or other driving forces that are probably subsumed under the "key trends" area.

In addition to this methodological critique, Quemey's BM shall be captured in its existing status quo at the moment. Hence, the need to analyze its environment will be greater when carrying the status quo forward into a future-oriented BM. For the same reason, the second step – generating the central platform idea with the **ideation canvas** – will be skipped, too. It is understood as pre-stage for the PVC, but here, its contents do not need to be developed anymore, only depicted.

Coming to the actual elements of the **PVC**, the first question is to determine the **four involved parties**. For Quemey this is particularly important, since they address multiple stakeholders, which raises the question who is "the customer".

- **Consumers**: Consumers are those who participate in Quemey's surveys, meaning air passengers who provide answers in the current survey pilots.
- **Producers**: "Producer" relates to the initiator, designer and orderer of surveys. Right now, Virgin Atlantic and GfK are such, since they ran surveys yet.
- **Owner**: Platform operator is Quemey, since they orchestrate the actions of all involved parties and assure a working ecosystem.
- **Partners**: Even though Virgin Atlantic and GfK have signed partnership contracts with Quemey, they are no partners in this definition. An actual partner is represented by e.g. the DTAG inflight team, as they facilitate the entire survey processing by providing internet access. A second partner would be LinkedIn, since they could improve Quemey's service with the enrichment of collected consumer data by LinkedIn user profile data. Nonetheless, e.g. GfK can in certain constellations also be considered as partner, in case they do not run a survey but help Quemey in terms of Go-to-Market support. Consequently, the sketched partner and producer roles in this platform BM are dynamic and hybrid roles. This counts also for LinkedIn: in the status quo, they are rather a partner, since they improve the basic platform services. Contrary to that, they become producers when running their own survey with Quemey.

Now that all stakeholders are captured in the PVC's outer circle, it follows the **value proposition** for each. According to Walter's instructions, each stakeholder needs to see a strong benefit, for the BM being able to work (Walter, Lohse, & Guzman, Platform Innovation Kit, 2017, S. 18). This covers pains and gains as well as jobs-to-be-done (terms known from Osterwalder et al.'s value proposition canvas (Osterwalder A. , Pigneur, Bernarda, & Smith, 2014, S. 8)):

- **Consumers**: As outlined at the beginning, the entire idea of Quemey is based on the thought that air passengers want to make better use of their flight time, instead of spending too much time unproductive, waiting for check in, boarding, and so forth. Thus, their value proposition is making better use of their time by being entertained with surveys in exchange for rewards.

- **Producers:** Surveying parties (Virgin Atlantic, GfK) are attracted by data on their topics of interest. A particular offering aspect is the access to customers in the air – a very encapsulated target group that is difficult to reach. Moreover, Quemey helps them with both survey development and evaluation.
- **Owner:** Quemey's first and foremost intention is to solve a relevant problem: they want people to make better use of their most valuable resource, namely their time. And Quemey wants to unleash the potential they see in their idea. Until now, they do not make money yet, so their key value is purpose. And they use all current activities to learn, which then enables them to thrive and grow.
- **Partners:** For DTAG, Quemey drives their Hot Spot product in terms of reputation, user acceptance and portfolio enrichment. In the long run, they also want to generate revenue thereby. As far as LinkedIn is concerned, they are a thoroughly data-driven business, and a platform business themselves, to the effect that they need to convince many users to increase their platform's attractiveness due to network effects. Hence, their benefit is increased usage and reach regarding their own platform, next to the obtained data which they can make money with from advertising, promising access to people in the air.

From these individual core value propositions, the respective **transactions** can be deduced. Altogether, there are no money flows included so far, since Quemey is still in a very early stage of development.

- **Consumers**: Air passengers are invited to participate in surveys, in which they provide their data, and they are rewarded with free WiFi as current incentive.
- **Producers**: The survey producers (Virgin Atlantic and GfK) bring into the system their survey cases, as well as their willingness to cooperate and to act as reference customers. In turn, they get consumer data from survey answers.
- **Owner**: Being the platform provider, Quemey acts as initiator and orchestrator, steering the activities with all involved parties. Therefore, Quemey receives strategic partnerships and support in realizing their idea.

- **Partners**: Quemey's current partners LinkedIn and DTAG's Hot Spot team have to be contemplated individually. First, the Hot Spot team assures internet access to enable a working survey infrastructure on board of aircrafts. Additionally, they support Quemey with their Go-to-Market approach, since they take them to relevant trade fairs or connect them with business contacts. In the current setting, the Hot Spot team receives the obtained data from the surveys they enable, at least in terms of demographic information. Second, LinkedIn allows Quemey to enrich their data with LinkedIn's user profile data, for which they are in turn integrated into Quemey's platform and processes.

Finally, the last remaining component of the PVC is about the **core value or mission** of the entire BM. It depicts a common connection between all involved parties, and all additional value propositions are supplied around this core (Walter, Lohse, & Guzman, Platform Innovation Kit, 2017, S. 18). For Quemey, this central value is compiled by combining the two most important unique values for the consumers' and producers' stakeholder groups: Quemey is the first company worldwide conducting incentivized surveys in the air, for passengers to make better use of their time, and for survey producers to get access to target group specific customer data.

Figure 5 summarizes the outlined points in Quemey's current BM, which was challenged and approved by Quemey's founders in a joint workshop.

Whereas this represents the core of Walter's platform business modelling methodology, in step four and five of its development process (see Table 1) a **platform service canvas and a platform strategy canvas** are suggested. Whilst the service canvas takes a closer look at the outlined transactions, the strategy canvas helps *"to define the playground when turning your idea into reality"* (Walter, Lohse, & Guzman, Platform Innovation Kit, 2017, S. 23). Accordingly, they are rather considered as operational and market introduction related, respectively. To keep the focus on conceptualization before implementation, they are not completed for the status quo, but will be for Quemey's future-oriented BM, when the question rises how to implement it successfully.

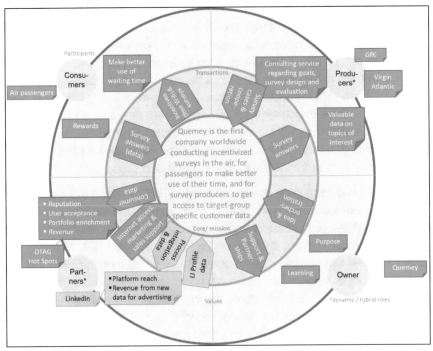

Figure 5: Quemey's Current Business Model
Source: own representation of the author based on (Walter, Lohse, & Guzman, Platform Innovation Kit, 2017, S. 18); the colour distinction in the partners' dimension represents corresponding elements for DTAG or LinkedIn, respectively; the sticker size does not represent any weighting or emphasis

3.2.2 Empiric Validation

3.2.2.1 Customer Interviews

„Fail fast, fail early, fail often" (Basulto, 2012, S. 1). In innovation management, failure is more and more considered an enrichment rather than something negative. From an economic point of view, innovations depict the realization of a business idea into a market success (Pleschak & Sabisch, 1996, S. 1). And ultimately, only customers determine market success by the degree of adoption for the respective innovation. Therefore,

(customer) feedback does not only improve the results, but also acceler-
ates the entire innovation cycle by faster identification of wrong ways, increased passion for innovating and improved agility when the overcoming
of obstructions is concerned (Sander, 2007, S. 99).

Against this backdrop, Quemey's current BM shall be validated, in order to
determine its current level of acceptance, and to be able to deduce respective challenges which are to be cured with the future-oriented BM. Since
Quemey addresses multiple stakeholders simultaneously, their acceptance is technically to be validated not only with "customers" (as defined in the common understanding) but also with producers and partners.
Since Quemey already initiated talks and even signed partnership contracts with the latter (GfK, Virgin Atlantic, DTAG and LinkedIn), it is assumed there is a general acceptance and trust in Quemey's BM existing.
Hence, the following validation will mainly concentrate on consumers:[6] air
passengers who are potential survey respondents.

In chapter 2.3.4 and 2.3.5, the chosen Mixed Methods design with its combination of first rather qualitative customer interviews and second a more
quantitative survey was presented. As far as the customer interviews are
concerned, Ash Maurya's problem and solution interview advice was chosen as starting point to derive the **interview questionnaire**. But as Quemey already detected a customer problem (too much waiting time) and
even developed a corresponding solution yet (making better use of time by
completing surveys in exchange for incentives), problem and solution interview are combined in one common interview guideline here with the following content: after collecting basic demographic information, the recommended "frame" introduces into the topic by stating that people are travelling more and more, and spend much time with waiting. At this point, it is
to be checked whether the interviewee perceives waiting as a problem.
Next, it is asked whether taking part in surveys instead of waiting would be
a potential alternative, in order to ascertain the concrete user acceptance
for Quemey's solution. Then, comparable to Maurya's pricing test, a sec-

---

[6] Consumers (party of platform value canvas) and customers (commonly used term in Lean
Startup literature) are used synonymously in the following.

tion on rewards follows, to find out which kind of rewards is preferred. Finally, a short summary rounds the interview guideline off, which is attached in Table 4. Special emphasis was put on asking for any further open comments, to discover the individual interviewee's thoughts as deeply as possible, again underlining the rather qualitative character of these interviews. The entire guideline has been refined with both Quemey founders in an iterative workshop approach, to make sure the available interview time can be used in the most effective and efficient way possible.

Table 4: Airport Interview Guideline

Date: 13.05.2017	Start time:	End time:
1. COLLECT DEMOGRAPHICS		
"Thanks for your openness. Before we start, I'd like to learn a little more about you…"		
Gender		
Age		
Job		
Travel Reason		
Target Location		
Avg. Ratio Business / Private Flights		
2. TELL A STORY		
"Great, thank you. So, let me explain you the context of what we're gonna talk about…"		
We frequently take flights from one place to another and spend most of our travel time with waiting. In consequence, we waste our most valuable asset: our time. Does that resonate with you?		
3. DEMO		
"Fine. Imagine you've checked in and wait for boarding."		
What annoys you most?		
What would you like to do instead?		
Would you fill in rewarded surveys during your waiting time?		

"Now imagine you're in the air, waiting for the plane to arrive."	
What annoys you most?	
What would you like to do instead?	
Would you fill in rewarded surveys during your waiting time?	
4. TEST REWARD	
"Now let's imagine you'd take part in such a market research survey..."	
What would be your preferred reward?	
Would you prefer immediate over downstream rewards?	
Would you prefer tangible (real) over intangible (virtual) rewards?	
5. WRAPPING UP	
"Many thanks for your answers – they're of great help!..."	
Is there anything else you'd like to add?	

Source: own representation of the author based on (Maurya, Running Lean. Iterate from Plan A to a Plan That Works, 2012, S. 85) and (Maurya, Running Lean. Iterate from Plan A to a Plan That Works, 2012, S. 103); slightly adopted

Regarding the interview **setting**, all interviews were conducted on a Saturday (13.05.2017) at Frankfurt Airport, Germany. This airport was assumed to provide the best mixture of long and short distance as well business and economy passengers. In line with the interview clues from 2.3.4, face-to-face interviews were chosen, mainly in a 1:1 setting (in exceptions, when e.g. a couple was travelling together, they were interviewed jointly). In essence, the interview team, compiled by five interviewers to prevent interviewer effects, randomly approached foreign air passengers at different airport locations (arrival hall, airport train station, business lounge). In total, 39 interviews were conducted, following the advice of approaching a huge, unspecified target group of 30-60 persons. Moreover, the recommendation of instant documentation was realized by taking notes in the interview guideline sheet, whereas recording was deliberately avoided as the interviewees might be suspicious towards voice recording. The participants were not incentivized but made aware that the interviews were taken for a university project. All interviewers were instructed to use the interview guideline as flexible instrument, to react accordingly to each individual interview flow, also in terms of English or German language. Moreover, the interviewers particularly encouraged their interviewees to come up with as many ideas as possible when open questions or any further comments at the end of each conversation were concerned.

After the interviews, the documentation sheets of all interviewers were collected, scanned and transferred to an excel **evaluation** sheet. First, the plain answers were copied – later, they were standardized to allow for higher comparability and to build categories of e.g. similar reward groups. This standardization increased objectivity in the evaluation, comparable to the intention of Mayring's qualitative content analysis (see 2.3.7). To a certain degree, this converted the outcome of qualitatively conceptualized interviews into quantitatively comparable results.

The evaluation showed that the interviewed target group is composed of 38% female and 62% male respondents. The age distribution is well-balanced, except for the group of 0-19 years with 5% only – which fits to the fact that market research does usually not address children, since their parents make the buying decisions. Both private and business passengers were met, although only 30% were business passengers,[7] probably due to the chosen weekend day.

Moving on to the **findings** on general user acceptance, 87% of all responses approved the "waiting" feeling during air journeys. Here and in the following, both "yes" and "sometimes" or "maybe" answers are interpreted as approval, since also "sometimes" or "maybe" express a general willingness, even though depending on the situational conditions. Before boarding, 80% of all respondents answered they would fill in surveys, and during the flight, even 92% would potentially do so. In this context, the influence of the flight distance was determined with 41% preferring long distance,

---

[7] Technically, interviewees were asked whether they fly more for business purpose or as private persons. Most respondents chose either business or private, 3% chose both.

18% short distance and 41% would participate on both long and short distance. Concerning the rewards that passengers would wish to receive, numerous suggestions were made. This indicates a preference for personalized rewards, meeting the individual air passengers' expectations. It was also tested whether passengers want immediate or downstream, and tangible or intangible incentives. Immediate was chosen by 67%, whereas 28% would take both and only 5% wished for downstream rewards. Beyond that, 44% prefer tangible rewards, 41% answered both and 15% chose intangible.

All in all, this allows the conclusion that air passengers expressed a high general user acceptance regarding Quemey's current and central idea to make better use of one's flight time. Looking at the provided rewards, representing a concrete matter of Quemey's product design if you will, it turned out that air passengers wish for personalized incentives, which in consequence brings the need to determine the individual reward preferences to comply the users' expectations. Particularly valuable insights could be derived from the additional comments at the end of the interviews. Amongst other things, they revealed that exciting topics can motivate as well, that another or a subproblem of waiting time is often a lack of information regarding e.g. delays, or that maybe a working and wellness area at the airport could be interesting to bridge waiting time. Figure 6 visualizes what was just described verbally.

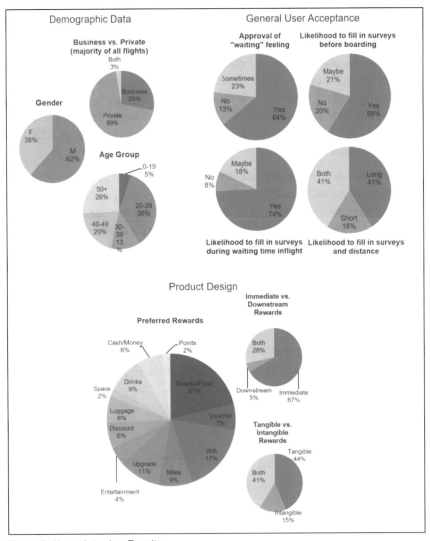

Figure 6: Airport Interview Results
Source: own representation of the author based on the obtained airport interview findings

3.2.2.2 Customer Survey

To validate the positive feedback on general user acceptance from the interviews with a larger audience and to exclude methodology-related effects, an online survey follows in step two of the pursued Mixed Methods approach. For this, the survey results shall be compared with the obtained interview results, which only allows for valid conclusions if the **questionnaire** from the airport interviews is used for the survey, too. Only slight adaptations were made regarding the detailedness of explanation, since during the survey there is no possibility to intervene in case of lacking information. For the same reason, additional free text fields were added, asking "why" the individual answer was chosen. This was intended to allow for open comments, as it is assumed that open (qualitative) answers enable even deeper findings than selecting from already existing options. Nonetheless, all "why" questions were not mandatory, because participants should not be annoyed by too many free text questions. Likewise, the reward section was modified: the participant was asked to select from a given range of proposed incentives, which originated from the interview answers. For further suggestions, a free text field for other ideas was appended. The survey questionnaire was again refined in an iterative workshop approach with Quemey's founders, to work out the optimum balance of comparability to the airport interviews and consideration of the particularities of online surveys. Its technical implementation (design and execution) was realized via a free student access to umfrageonline.com.

As stated in chapter 2.3.5, conducting surveys via the internet offers the main advantage that a **larger audience** can be reached with lower effort. This was considered very beneficial in the present case, since altogether 402 completed surveys could be collected. This was reached by promoting the survey via various online communities, such as different Facebook groups, all Facebook and LinkedIn contacts of Quemey's founders as well as of the author, and the contacts of third parties who shared the survey invitation themselves. Further, XING and Twitter were used to raise awareness, and eventually the survey was also promoted via the supervising university Hochschule Bonn-Rhein-Sieg. Altogether, a different target group mixture than the interviews was reached: with 72% belonging to the age group of 20-29, there is no balanced age situation anymore. In contrast to the interviews, also the gender shares are inverted, with 41% male and 59% female respondents. And only one fifth are rather business passengers.

As a whole, the **survey results** managed to confirm and further substantiate the conclusions drawn from the interviews, although with slight percentage differences. Analyzed in predominantly the same style as the interviews, 89% approved a certain "waiting feeling" during flights. 90% answered they would fill in surveys during they wait for boarding, whereas 81% would do so during their flight time. The likelihood to participate in a Quemey survey also tends to be higher on long distance flights (24%) than on short distances (8%), whilst for the largest percentage of 68% it makes no difference. Similar to the interviews, downstream rewards (5%) are less preferred than immediate ones (52%), and once more a huge number of respondents is indifferent (43%). Next, 33% chose tangible rewards, 11% intangible ones, and 56% would take both. And again, the surveyed participants answered very heterogeneously on reward categories, which reinforces the conclusion that they need to be personalized.

In addition to these largely quantitative results as condensed in Figure 7, many interesting thoughts were found in the additional comments. Some participants stated that the air conditioning is often too cold, that the aircraft sounds are too noisy, that the entire process design is poorly organized or that the seats are too small. Thus, huge potential for operators regarding service improvement can be inferred. As far as the reasoning comments which explain the participants' answers are concerned: they correspond with the broad range of preferred rewards without any observable common trends amongst the respondents. This proves that each air passenger has individual perceptions and preferences, which underlines the need for personalization.

To draw an overarching conclusion of this empirical validation: Quemey's idea was approved, as both the airport interviews and the survey attested a high user acceptance. In addition, both instruments indicated a general preference of a personalized product/ service design. This opens up possibilities for improvement, particularly for the provided incentives. Especially open answers and additional comments were very instructive, as they entailed lots of interesting thoughts or comparisons with great travel experiences. All these insights are now condensed in Quemey's current challenges, and thought ahead in a scenario analysis.

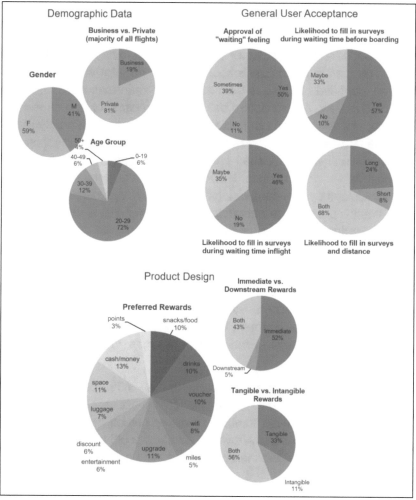

Figure 7: Survey Results
Source: own representation of the author, based on the obtained customer survey findings

3.3 Challenges and Perspectives

3.3.1 Current Challenges

Composing Quemey's current challenges shall happen in a systematic way, to prevent listing them randomly. Thus, Quemey's current BM as depicted in Figure 5 is taken as starting point and frame. The findings from airport interviews, survey and additional deep dive interviews with Quemey's founders and further experts serve as input to highlight challenging aspects or open issues. In the light of Mayring's **qualitative content analysis**, all identified challenges from the expert interviews have been collected inductively. As mentioned before, no software solution chosen for doing so, since the broad range of diverse topics is not sufficiently standardizable. Instead, a "**light version**" was applied, meaning the interview documentations were screened and challenge categories were inferred with post its and text markers. Having done so, the detected categories were scrutinized by screening all interviews again for points that contribute to the identified challenge categories. In consequence, a combination of inductive and deductive categorizing was used and its overall outcome captured in
Figure 8.

In the following, all derived challenges will be examined in the sequence of steps in which the BM was developed in chapter 3.2.1. When doing so, not each and every single statement from the expert interviews will be named – instead they will be aggregated to key messages, to avoid getting lost in a maze.

Starting with the **challenges observable in the PVC dimensions** (Figure 5), two main challenges could be identified for the **stakeholder** circle. First, Quemey should enlarge the number of involved parties, particularly regarding producers and partners. Above all, partners could enable the integration into IFEC systems and thereby make survey participation even more convenient.

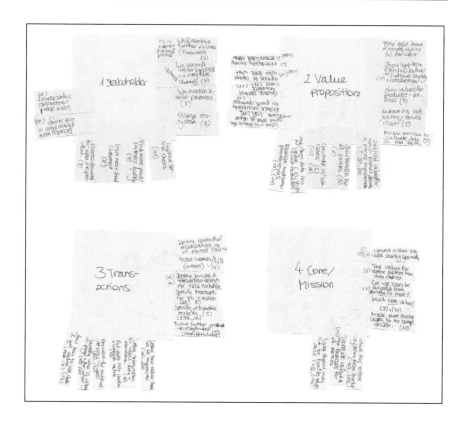

Figure 8: Qualitative Content Analysis of Expert Interviews: Challenges
Source: own representation of the author based on expert interviews; each post it contains
a statement of an expert interview, equipped with the number of the respective interview, in
order to make their sources as transparent as possible

Other than that, Quemey needs to extend the demand side of their multi-sided platform market model by winning more survey producers, since platform businesses always need to balance out the forces of demand and supply. In addition, Quemey faces the challenge to understand each addressed stakeholder's motives, needs, concerns and worries, to identify what they want.

Moving on to the second circle of the PVC, it turned out that the key challenge is to identify, communicate and realize a convincing **value** for each party. Even though the current BM already offers first suggestions for provided values, they are neither exhaustive nor thoroughly thought through. For consumers for example, Quemey needs to identify their individual preferences, to be able to establish a survey and incentive matching process, and to pave the way for further improvements in e.g. customer experience during their journey. As extrapolated from the interview and survey comments, this is an existing and important pain. Other than that, the PVC names new data as value proposition for the producers. In this context, particularly the expert interviews underlined that data themselves are no actual value. Hence, Quemey needs to identify value propositions and use cases that can actually bring additional value, and which ultimately result in financial success or other overarching objectives such as customer satisfaction or loyalty. The same counts for partners: especially the aircraft interior suppliers, who are not won as partners yet, have to be convinced with powerful values. The value propositions for existing partners should be refined likewise. Finally, Quemey themselves will not continue their endeavours for purpose and learnings forever. Therefore, another challenge is to actually make money.

Third, in the **transaction** dimension, Quemey has not specified a contractual conditions model yet, which standardizes all exchange relationships. Eventually the entire transaction design of the current BM displays a lack of detail. At first, this concerns the exchange processes between consumers and the platform, since no survey and incentive matching process is established yet. Further, producers need more than just plain data. They need advice how to turn the collected data into valuable insights, thus these consulting services need to be added in the producer transactions. In general, and regarding all involved parties, there is no monetization model developed so far. This was noted by some experts, leading to the question who will be charged and which monetization model will be determined. Once more this underlines the need for powerful values, for their receivers to develop a certain willingness to pay.

Finally, the centre of the PVC points out Quemey's current **core value or mission**. Right now, it is the idea of conducting surveys during air journeys, as the first solution worldwide that offers data demanders the access to this encapsulated target group. Here, Quemey faces the challenge to evolve their core value towards the data sharing vision, which both founders of Quemey share and believe in. To actually realize this, a strong value add for each involved party needs to be found (which should also lead to financial success from data sharing).

In addition to the analyzed PVC dimensions derived from Quemey's current BM (Figure 5), the expert interviews as well as the free text comments from airport interviews and online survey led to **new defiances** Quemey should consider:

The first challenge category is the **implementation challenge**. Quemey's founders could list nearly endless ideas for their business. "Think big, start small, scale fast" has become a common mantra of entrepreneurs – it counts for Quemey, too: they face the challenge to realize their transactions technically, to assure e.g. hygiene factors or preconditions such as data security, or compliance of legal requirements. Further, online survey, airport and expert interviews equally emphasized the importance of a data access control option for consumers, to avoid a feeling of being controlled and instead make them feel an own control power.

Challenge category number two is the **environmental challenge**, meaning Quemey should analyze their environment with all relevant actors. They should investigate current industry and societal trends and assess to which degree they impact Quemey's activities. Further, they should take a closer look at their competitive landscape. On one hand, this might show best practice approaches and bring new impulses. On the other hand, it helps to recognize competitive threats.

This leads to the third category: the **uniqueness challenge**. Right now, Quemey has built a SaaS platform service to realize their idea, and they could convince first partners and survey producers. Nonetheless, there are no entry barriers for potential copycat competitors. Quemey needs to identify a certain differentiator, or they have to become the biggest platform player with this business purpose, since platform markets tend to be "winner takes it all" markets.

To become a big monopolistic platform player, Quemey needs to scale. This is called the **scaling challenge**, requesting sufficient manpower, time, knowledge and money, but also a huge ecosystem of involved stakeholders, constituting a certain market power. Moreover, Quemey's entire value chain is to be developed from a manufactory to a scalable, well-defined process design.

To be able to acquire sufficient resources to scale their business, one precondition is that Quemey achieves a self-sustaining business case, titled the **business case challenge**. Once more, this implies the urgency of finding a monetization model, to help Quemey to actually make money.

In Table 5, a compressed version of the just described aspects is provided, reducing Quemey's current challenges to their quintessences.

Table 5: Quemey's Current Challenges

Challenge Categories	Challenges
1 Stake-holders	• Not enough producers & partners integrated • No exhaustive understanding of each party's world & interests
2 Value Proposi-tions	→ no powerful values identified, transported & realized for each party yet • **Consumers**: no identification of individual interests yet, in order to personalize survey topics, rewards, or to improve service design • **Producers**: no detailed understanding what more data will improve & how they can be converted into value • **Owner**: no financial values recognizable yet • **Partners**: no integration into aircraft on-board systems yet, hence no values for suppliers defined, and other values should be refined

3 Transactions	→ no contractual conditions model for exchange relationships defined yet • **Consumers**: no survey topic & incentive matching process defined • **Producers**: no money flows & pricing models developed, no concrete transactions for co-creation, consulting & data evaluation specified • **Owner**: no money flows yet • **Partners**: no integration into aircraft on-board systems yet, hence no concrete transaction design defined (also for other partners)
4 Core / Mission	• Convert vision from survey approach into data sharing approach with additional values resulting for all parties involved
General Challenges	• Environment challenge • Implementation challenge • Scaling challenge • Uniqueness challenge • Business case challenge

Source: own representation of the author, based on conclusions from airport interviews (3.2.2.1), survey (3.2.2.2), and expert interviews

3.3.2 Future Perspectives

„...*recipes should not be routinely followed; rather, they should be changed altogether when appropriate and necessary*" (Wright & Cairns, 2011, S. 3). In this spirit, it is not sufficient to derive current challenges from the analysis of Quemey's current BM. On the contrary, the scenario analysis methodology shall now help to collate future challenges resulting from possible scenarios. The intention behind doing so was already hinted – here pointed out more precisely: the obtained future perspectives, trends and challenges shall be taken up when developing Quemey's future-oriented BM in the next chapter.

Scenario analysis was introduced as a methodology that helps to understand the future and prepare for it accordingly, also emotionally. It integrates threats, opportunities and other influence factors to recognize future trends, to empower decision making or derive required actions. In the following, Günther's **scenario analysis procedure** (goal determination (1), environment analysis (2), scenario creation (3), vision development (4), options for action (5), implementation (6) (Günther, no release date specified, S. 1)) shall act as an initial starting point, though it will be slightly adjusted, resulting from the following train of thought:

As the previous course of the analysis showed, Quemey operates a **multi-sided platform market**. In general, a platform owner is obliged to make sure that the number of suppliers is equivalent to the number of demanders, since there is a dependent relationship between the two (or their offers and requests). If there are for example too many vendors on a sales platform, this leads to excess supply and a shortage of customers, which then causes a price drop, and the attractiveness of the platform quickly declines either. If the platform owner does not intervene, this might end in a downward spiral (Clement & Schreiber, 2016, S. 264-265). In contrast to one-sided markets, the equilibrium price on multi-sided markets is not only determined by the existing price structure, but also by interactions between groups of users or demanders (Clement & Schreiber, 2016, S. 266). Thus, it appears that the development of a multi-sided market is to a large extent depending on the respective demand and supply development.

Transferring this thought to the present platform business – Quemey – it follows that their future is heavily influenced by the development of data demand and data supply. More accurately, in their current BM they depend on the development of data demand from producers and partners with a need for consumer information and on corresponding data supply from consumers who participate in a survey. Taking these two factors – data demand from producers and partners, and data supply from consumers – as axes of a scenario graph, **four scenarios emerge** as a function of data demand and data supply (Figure 9). Below, each scenario will be explained briefly and matched with a strategy recommendation:

- If air passengers are very likely to participate in surveys during flights, the high data supply feeding into Quemey's data base results in a huge amount of data and thus user profiles. This strong core asset depicts a good basis for negotiations with new partners and producers. Simultaneously, if producers and partners know that there is a very high consumer acceptance and participation rate, not only Quemey's existing data, but also the possibility to launch their own surveys is very appealing to them. Resulting from these new surveys, Quemey's data base is growing and growing. Hence, this scenario is called "**self-reinforcing growth**", and Quemey should exploit the opportunity of supportive data demanders and data suppliers to let their business grow. Moreover, this represents ideal conditions for Quemey to claim money for their services, in order to realize a self-sustaining business case.

- On the opposite, if consumers do not want to disclose their personal data, and if there are no producers or partners with a need for data, poor prospects for Quemey are the result. If consumers do not provide data, Quemey's data base will stay small, to the effect that they have a weak negotiating position when aspiring to attract new producers and partners. A little number of producers and partners causes a little number of surveys, no new data, and no new consumers who spread good word of mouth, which again weakens the chances to acquire new participants. Monetization seems nearly impossible in this case. Consequently, this scenario is called "**unattractive downward spiral**", associated with the recommendation to leave the market, since every new activity creates new effort without any perspectives on a pay-off.

- Both presented scenarios showed a balance between supply and demand – either both high or both low. Remembering the responsibility of a platform owner to adjust imbalances, the next two scenarios deal with either excess demand or excess supply situations. If consumers are again positive towards disclosing their data in surveys, but if the demand from the producers' and partners' perspective is simply not existing, Quemey has nobody they can sell their data to, to put it simply. "**Disequilibrium due to excess data supply**" seems an appropriate labelling for this scenario. In this case, Quemey should stimulate the demand side of the market. If they manage to do so, there will be more producers and partners conducting surveys, they will meet fruitful ground regarding open-minded consumers who participate, leading to a larger data base, and the upward spiral into the direction of self-reinforcing growth will hopefully start. If this works, Quemey could also think about monetization.

- Ultimately, it remains the situation where producers and partners have a high demand for data, but consumers are unlikely to reveal their personal data. Again, an imbalance follows: a "**disequilibrium due to excess data demand**". Comparable to the previous scenario, Quemey should initiate a movement towards the upward spiral by stimulating consumer data supply.

Figure 9 summarizes what was just explained. Altogether, three scenarios show business opportunities for Quemey and are therefore shaded.

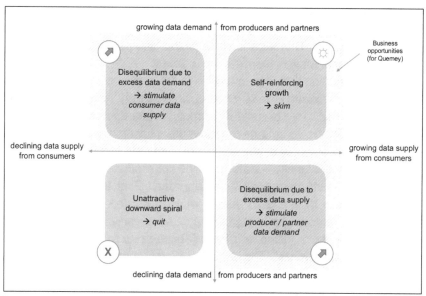

Figure 9: Future Scenarios for Quemey's Current Business Model
Source: own representation of the author

This being sad, the above thoughts are not sufficient here, as they only perpetuate Quemey's current model into the future. Since Quemey aims at realizing their vision of a data sharing approach, data supply from consumers is not the only source that brings data into the system. Following this logic, the dimension of data supply from producers/ partners needs to be added, indicating their willingness to grant other parties access to their own data bases. A **three-dimensional model with new scenarios emerges** (Figure 10), which simultaneously shows that platform businesses lead to the necessity of new supply demand considerations. To focus on the most essential, only those four situations are analyzed that show actual business opportunities for Quemey, pictured in the marked cube:

- Starting with the best case once more, high data demand and high data supply would represent the optimal situation. This is marked as "**sweet spot**", where Quemey has a large data base (now fed from both consumers, and producers/ partners) and the respective demand, hence they only need to turn their data into value. Reaching this sweet spot by targeted actions is proposed to be Quemey's strategic goal in all other scenarios. This situation was called "self-reinforcing growth" before, with best future prospects for Quemey.
- Another situation that is comparable to the previous scenario model is the "**disequilibrium due to excess data supply**". Again, Quemey is recommended to systematically stimulate data demand from producers and partners, to actuate the movement towards the sweet spot.
- Next, the data supply dimension is split into data supply from consumers and – additionally – data supply from producers and partners in form of the envisaged data sharing approach. First, lacking data supply from consumers is a case that is known from the previous scenario model. To anchor the described split also verbally, this scenario's name is slightly modified to "**disequilibrium due to lack of data supply from consumers**". The strategy recommendation stays the same: the lacking factor of consumer data supply is to be stimulated.
- It remains the "new" scenario "**disequilibrium due to lack of data supply from producers/ partners**". For now, this is assumed to be the most challenging scenario for Quemey, since it means unknown territory. It stands to reason that Quemey should stimulate the data supply from producers and partners, to steer their business into the promising direction of the sweet spot.

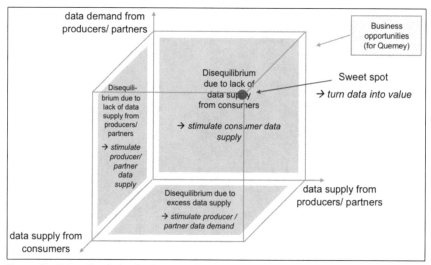

Figure 10: Future Scenarios for Potential Data Sharing Business Model
Source: own representation of the author

Having drawn this picture, the question rises **which scenario is expected**. To systematically assess the probabilities of occurrence in an objectively comprehensive manner, a valuation model would be needed. This is estimated a large task which goes beyond the scope of what this project can deliver. But it is assumed that each effective force requires a certain degree of stimulation, to push Quemey towards the sweet spot. This special point represents a perfect situation, ne plus ultra, a nearly utopian state. Thus, it will always be necessary to actively influence the active forces, to bring Quemey closer to this optimum. So how can data demand and data supply can be influenced? This particular question was investigated with the interviewed experts, as shown in Figure 11.

Figure 11: Qualitative Content Analysis of Expert Interviews: Perspectives
Source: own representation of the author based on expert interviews

In the same style like for the current challenges, a **qualitative content analysis** was applied here. Since the technique was described in detail when discussing Quemey's current challenges, this section will not do so repeatedly and instead concentrate on the main findings from its application. The expert statements on the pursued question could be classified to the three stimulation strategies resulting from the above scenario description, as summarized and briefly explained in Table 6. Altogether, this list does not claim to be exhaustive, but provides recommendations for a first set of helpful steps, empowering Quemey to take action.

Table 6: Recommended Actions for Developed Stimulation Strategies

Stimulation Strategies	Recommended Actions
1 Stimulate producer/ partner data demand	▪ **Show value** from Quemey's data & services, particularly for product improvement & process improvements, with use cases, references & industry trends – finally resulting in financial success ▪ **Increase contacts** & producers/ partners to acquire more demanders ▪ **Grow data base & business** for a stronger negotiating & market position ▪ **Eliminate barriers** regarding technical & contractual uncertainties
2 Stimulate consumer data supply	▪ **Show own benefits** from data provisioning like contribution to improved products & services or less waiting time ▪ **Personalize** survey topics & incentives ▪ **Establish trust** by e.g. opt out/ control options about data, assured data privacy & market reputation ▪ **Reach more consumers** by e.g. new surveys, advertising, word of mouth ▪ **Eliminate barriers** regarding effort to participate (e.g. with no fees for consumers, no annoying processes, test participation), or regarding intransparent conditions
3 Stimulate producer/ partner data supply	▪ **Show value from sharing** resulting from returns or participation models, e.g. with use cases, references & industry trends ▪ **Increase contacts**, talk to potential producers & partners to understand their worlds, to co-create & to acquire more potential suppliers

	• **Encourage respective mind-set** that sharing is to the greater good of the entire community, jointly with politics & education • **Eliminate barriers** regarding expected weakening from sharing, legal, technical & contractual uncertainties

Source: own representation of the author based on expert interviews

Bottom line, this shows that the **most important recommendations** are again about transporting strong values for each party, next to growing Quemey's entire platform system and eliminating disturbing factors like e.g. legal, technological and contractual uncertainties. All these recommendations have to be contemplated against the backdrop of Quemey's **environment**. For now, Quemey mainly addresses the aviation industry, which is why the key trends and changes of the aviation industry should be taken into account, although they are not treated as extensively as the stimulation strategies, since Quemey has a relatively little influence on them. For commercial aviation, PwC identified two main driving forces, which are *"the use of digital technologies and the development of sharper, more nuanced competitive positioning"* (Bohlman, Kletzel, & Terry, 2017, S. 5). Other than that, Bombardier published in their commercial aircraft market forecast five key trends for the next 20 years: Reduced yields per passenger, more intra-regional routes, higher usage of smaller aircrafts, maximization of profit per passenger and the replacement of resource-intensive aircrafts (Bombardier, 2017, S. 1-3). All these points have in common that they cause major changes for the industry, whether it be digital transformation, increasing competition or making processes more effective and efficient. To cope with these changes, all market participants need information and advice – encouraging the need for data and services as provided by Quemey.

Expanding these thoughts towards the aspired data sharing BM, also key drivers of the entire travel, transport and logistics industry are to be considered. Depending on the interviewed experts' knowledge domains, these drivers were partly incorporated into their statements already. To accentuate them, the main trends for the travel sector are briefly illustrated as published by McKinsey in 2017. According to their findings, the relationship between people and data is changing, meaning that data can make powerful recommendations, but in the end humans decide whether they accept new things or not. And although more and more data are generated and evaluable by new skilled data scientists and the like – it still requires business expertise to derive the right decisions. Thinking about the human dimension is relevant for customers as well, with personalization being another main trend (Bowcott, 2017, S. 2-5). All in all, it can be summarized that the right combination of data (incl. corresponding analytics capabilities) and business expertise helps to stay competitive in the future. Both things are at the core of Quemey's value proposition and their database as their main asset, which should be embedded into consulting and reporting services. Hence, these external trends are not directly influenceable, but provide a fruitful and supporting environment for the core problems Quemey addresses.

Altogether, if comparing these identified future perspectives and the respective action recommendations with the previously discussed current challenges, it is noticeable that they are not entirely free from **overlaps**. Remembering what was stated as meta goal, namely solving the research question in a pragmatic, rather than highly sophisticated way, this is not rated a major problem. The main thing is that all identified challenges and future expectations are taken up and provided with a sound answer in Quemey's future-oriented BM.

Finally, looking back at Günther's scenario analysis procedure model (Günther, no release date specified, S. 1), it remains to turn the recommended actions into reality. This cannot be done on paper, but to make a first step into this direction, the following section absorbs all findings into a potential future BM for Quemey.

3.4 Future-oriented Data Sharing Business Model

3.4.1 Development

Ultimately, all ingredients that the **BM creation formula** (Figure 12) suggests have been collected. Quemey's current BM was sketched and validated with potential users in airport interviews as well as in a subsequent online survey. With the help of expert interviews, current challenges were developed and a scenario analysis revealed further future perspectives.

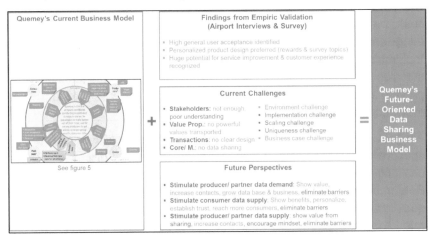

Figure 12: Future-oriented Business Model Creation Formula
Source: own representation of the author based on previous tables and figures

Hence, the core topic can be tackled now: it is time to put all findings together and develop Quemey's future-oriented data sharing BM. To do so, the current BM (Figure 5) is taken as starting point, to the effect that Walter's PVC will be used again. The previously collected PVC contents are reviewed, modified and supplemented by further aspects, which could be deduced from the listed ingredients. The resulting future-oriented BM proposal was challenged and refined in a joint workshop with Quemey's founders. To make transparent which elements have been modified or added newly (compared to the current BM), a colour distinction was included. The final outcome is featured in Figure 13 and will now be explained in depth.

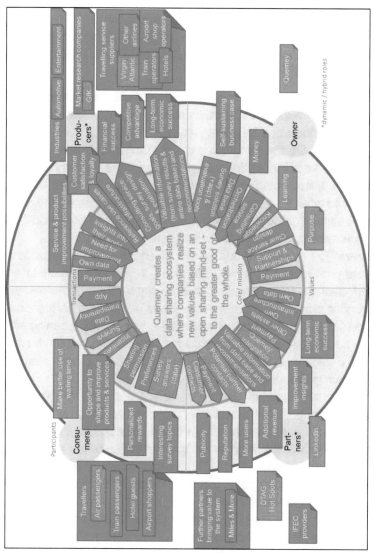

Figure 13: Quemey's Future-oriented Business Model
Source: own representation of the author based on (Walter, Lohse, & Guzman, Platform Innovation Kit, 2017, S. 18); blue stickers originate from the current business model descrip-tion in Figure 5; green stickers have been modified or newly added; again, the size of the stickers does not represent any weighting or emphasis

It is obvious on the first sight, that the picture is crowded with stickers, showing that many new aspects could be identified.Starting with the outer circle and relevant **stakeholder groups**, it becomes obvious that the number of stakeholders has increased:

- **Consumers**: Coming from air passengers as initial consumer group, new consumer groups such as train passengers, hotel guests, airport shoppers and others can be addressed when extending Quemey's approach to the entire travelling value chain. Altogether, these consumers can be summarized as "travellers", who can take different roles (as just described) according to their current activity or the used service. This has two effects: a larger total number of consumers, and more information about these consumers, since they are contemplated from various viewpoints according to their current role now.
- **Producers**: The producer group mirrors what was outlined for consumers. More producing actors from the entire travelling value chain are included, such as train operators, hotels, airport shop operators and other service providers. Their participation is understood as precondition to realize the outlined consumer effects. Next to these participants from the travel, transport and logistics industry, market research companies like GfK or other industries like automotive or entertainment show interest in Quemey's offering already.
- **Owner**: Quemey remains platform operator and owner – the only stakeholder group that is stable in comparison to Quemey's current BM. However, their role evolves from a pure data collector and transferor to an information broker, in the understanding of the term which was described in chapter 2.1.2. This means Quemey translates the shared data into a format that is comprehensible for the receiving party, and they interpret them for the receiving party.
- **Partners**: Next to the existing partners LinkedIn and the DTAG Hot Spot team, especially IFEC providers should become part of Quemey's ecosystem, as outlined previously. Moreover, further partners should be convinced and selected based on the premise that they bring a certain value into the system, for the entire system's value to increase and consequently for these partners to benefit from the entire system's

value in turn. Miles & More for example constitutes a promising partner, as found in both airport interviews and survey.

Second, the central issue in the **value proposition** dimension was to identify and communicate powerful values for each stakeholder group. As becomes obvious from the Figure 13, the number of value boxes has proliferated[8]:

- **Consumers**: Here, Quemey started with the idea that consumers want to make better use of their time. In the future, there are more value propositions: consumers are provided with interesting, entertaining survey topics and rewards that fit to their personal interests. Both surveys and rewards were listed as values in the current BM already, but as the airport interviews and the subsequent survey showed, both can provide even greater value when personalized. Further, consumers can actively shape products and services they use themselves by providing their opinion on these. This value could be of great meaning for consumers, too, depending on their individual motivating factors.
- **Producers**: Producers (originally of surveys) typically pursue economic interests, meaning they are attracted by values such as long-term economic prosperity, competitive advantage and financial success, resulting from customer satisfaction and loyalty. This is based on data, which – when evaluated and interpreted accordingly – allow for service and product improvement suggestions. Whereas Quemey's current BM raised data on relevant problems as central value, it became obvious that producers do not care about data for the sake of having more data, but for the thereby enabled economic success.
- **Owner**: Next to learning and purpose – Quemey's initial values – a sustainable BM requires a self-sustaining business case. Hence, an additional value for Quemey should be making money from their business idea.
- **Partners**: For partners, the same basic mind-set is assumed as for producers: they mainly pursue economic interests, to the effect that

---

[8] This is partly due to the fact that separate values are not summarized anymore, to sharpen and outline single value components. Nonetheless, many new values could be identified and added.

they are motivated by values such as publicity, reputation, increased user numbers and consequently additional revenue, supporting long-term economic success. Further, with access to Quemey's data eco-system they can – comparable to the producers – derive improvements for their own products and services.

Next, the **transaction** dimension translates these values into actual ex-change relationships. Once more, Figure 13 pictures that the number of transaction elements has increased. This takes up the identified challenge of uncertainty regarding the concrete transaction design, at least in a first step, which leaves room for further detailing when implementing the sketched BM in the next chapter.

- **Consumers**: The first required input for personalization are corre-sponding information on individual preferences. Having received these, Quemey can send out surveys to participants that mirror their individual interests (with the help of a survey-matching-process that is to be specified). Consumers then need to provide their survey answers, and they have to grant an individual sharing permit for all parties that can access their data. This takes up the identified wish for control – a critical prerequisite for consumer participation and willingness to share. The indication of preferences as well as control settings could be done via a Quemey app, making the entire survey processing including pre- and after-work even more user-friendly and convenient. In addition, this would facilitate a check who can access which of their data at all times, establishing a high degree of transparency.
- **Producers**: To enable Quemey to deliver valuable services, producers need to provide insights into their respective world, as well as a need for improvement that Quemey can solve with data and the correspond-ing services of e.g. use case identification, survey creation and evalu-ation. Additionally, in the data sharing approach producers need to contribute their own (customer) data or grant access to these, respec-tively. Besides, a form of payment for Quemey's services is required from the producers, since they receive value that should trigger a cer-tain payment motivation. As concluded from the expert interviews,

Quemey should not charge the consumers who pay with their data already, but rather producers who actually request these data. Though it is open how exactly the monetization model will look like, one should keep in mind that producers could also "pay" by granting access to their own data.

- **Owner**: To enable the entire system, Quemey's SaaS platform and survey solution is a fundamental precondition to operationally perform their surveys, as well as an appropriate and top-performing data base. Moreover, Quemey brings in knowledge to identify valuable data-based use cases, needed for their consulting services and overarching orchestration function. Finally, they have to provide a concrete and well-defined service design, for instance regarding the survey-matching-process or regarding the data-sharing-transactions. In turn, Quemey receives support and partnerships from the system, and ultimately also payment to empower a self-sustaining business case – implying the need to specify a monetization and pricing model, respectively.
- **Partners**: The partners bring in their infrastructure or other assets, helping Quemey to expand their offering and make it even more convenient. Against the data sharing background, the partners can also grant access to their own data. In exchange, they are integrated into Quemey's ecosystem and receive valuable information from their central data base, maybe even with targeted recommendations. As another consequence, they also get relevant contacts, allowing to realize the portrayed values of e.g. publicity or an extended user base. Potentially, even bidirectional payment could come into effect here.

Finally, it remains Quemey's **core value or mission**. Whilst their current BM focuses on the survey data idea, to make better use of the passengers' travel time, the future-oriented version it is not limited to this aspect anymore. It is enlarged, allowing for more powerful values: "Quemey creates a data sharing ecosystem where companies realize new values based on an open sharing mind-set – to the greater good of the whole" (Figure 13). This value proposition includes strong advantages for each party, and it puts the data sharing idea in the centre.

As this entire delineation shows, it takes up many of the identified challenges from the BM creation formula (Figure 12). Nonetheless, some questions remain open: how exactly can Quemey turn this business model into reality? This cannot be cured with a static BM description, but hopefully with the following section.

3.4.2 Implementation

"(...) Implementation is the most important stage of any major change effort" (Scott & Tesvic, 2014, S. 7). Hence, it shall be treated with special attention now. Having defined the core of Quemey's future-oriented BM with the help of Walter's PVC, the platform service canvas and the platform strategy canvas remain from his toolkit. Whereas the service canvas specifies the platform's core services to enable seamless engagement, matching and transaction handling, the strategy canvas paves the way for the BM realization itself (Walter, Lohse, & Guzman, Platform Innovation Kit, 2017, S. 20-23). Both canvases have been prefilled based on the findings as listed in the BM creation formula (Figure 12), and refined in a joint session with Quemey's founders, which feedbacked and approved their content.

Starting with the **service canvas** (Figure 14), it addresses the need for a clearly defined transaction and service design, as pointed out in Quemey's current challenges. Originally, it consists of three parts: on the right, it lists the stakeholder groups, whilst in the middle the components of engagement, matchmaking and transaction are specified, followed by the required activities, resources and technologies on the left (Walter, Lohse, & Guzman, Platform Innovation Kit, 2017, S. 20).

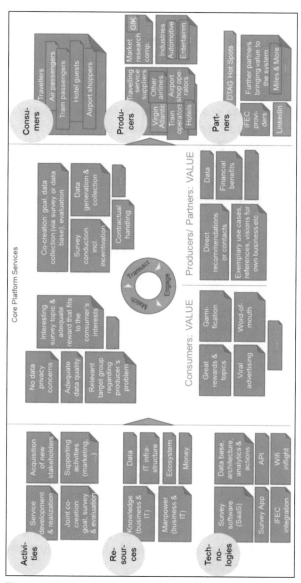

Figure 14: Quemey's Future-oriented Service Design
Source: own representation of the author based on (Walter, Lohse, & Guzman, Platform Innovation Kit, 2017, S. 20); again, the size of the stickers does not represent any weighting or emphasis

The **stakeholder groups** on the right remain constant compared to the PVC, hence they do not help to gain additional knowledge. For the services of **engagement** in the middle, consumers and producers/ partners should be differentiated, since they are attracted by different values. Consumers could be engaged with great rewards, viral advertising campaigns or peer recommendations, referring to the power of user reviews in the internet economy, since users trust their peers more than unknown service providers (Clement & Schreiber, 2016, S. 86-87). Moreover, consumers could be engaged by gamification elements in the proposed app, to fuel their motivation and make all activities more interesting (Werbach & Hunter, 2012, S. 44). It would be conceivable to design surveys as games or quizzes, or to add functions for points collection and recommendation of funny surveys to friends. Next, producers and partners are best engaged by their outlined values. Quemey could also become interesting by direct recommendations of business contacts, by presenting exemplary use cases and references or by sketching future visions for a company's business.

It succeeds the **matchmaking** of surveys and participants. Relevant factors that determine a successful matching are the target group definition of the survey producer, the consumer preferences on topics and rewards, the balance between participation effort and received incentive and the general reward attractiveness. Additionally, all data privacy concerns of the consumers should be complied, and high data quality is necessary to determine whether the mentioned factors fit.

Next, the main **transactions** for Quemey are the survey conduction itself, including the subsequent evaluation and interpretation of results, leading to concrete recommendations. This is linked to the data generation process, complemented by data collection from data sharing. An accompanying activity is depicted by the consulting or co-creation process, in which Quemey and a producer or partner jointly define their goal and their data collection process design, and evaluate it afterwards. All these steps are guided by a corresponding contractual handling.

In order to perform all these services, Quemey's core **activities** are service development and realization, stakeholder acquisition, co-creation and further supporting activities, such as marketing or financial planning. For these activities, Quemey needs certain **resources**, like knowledge and manpower, as well as a huge data base and scalable, performing IT infrastructure. To strengthen their negotiating power, they have to enlarge their overall ecosystem, helping them to grow towards the aspired monopolist position. Naturally, all these efforts require money to buy e.g. the necessary IT. Finally, Quemey's enabling **technologies** are their SaaS survey software, their data base with an effective and efficient IT architecture, corresponding analytics solutions, and ultimately components to turn the obtained findings into actions. Another recommended technology is the survey app, which bundles all consumer-related actions such as preference indication, control of data access and survey participation. Besides, inflight WiFi facilitates on-board survey participation (until the integration into IFEC systems).

Continuing with Walter's **strategy canvas**, it compiles influencing factors, and helps to define one's respective positioning and finally strategies to turn the aspired positioning into reality (Walter, Lohse, & Guzman, Platform Innovation Kit, 2017, S. 23-25).

The **influencing** aspects on the top layer start with the relevant stakeholders, which are known from the PVC. Next, the canvas continues with endogenous and exogenous business drivers. For Quemey, the expert interviews revealed that both companies and private persons face massive uncertainties when thinking about legal regulations on data privacy. This is reflected and partly reasoned by the ongoing legislative changes of the new EU General Data Protection Regulation, becoming effective in 2018. Regarding internal business drivers, the expert interviews mostly named the need to convey strong values for all involved parties, since those values decide whether they think about participating in Quemey's BM or not. Particular important aspects for consumers are CX and trust, which is why these two points are listed separately. Moving on, influence factor number three is competition. As analyzed with Quemey's founders, they operate in a very heterogeneous landscape with multiple competitors, each with different value propositions and BMs. But basically, they all extract value from data. Though, none of them unites the aspects Quemey combines: surveys to generate data, doing so in the travel, transport and logistics industry, creating a data sharing ecosystem and pursuing a co-creation mode in a platform setting. This shows that Quemey is different. But are they also uncopiable?

Layer two, the **positioning** layer starts with Quemey's vision, taking up the ExO concept as presented earlier: "Quemey is a disruptive and growing partner for companies, helping them to generate and analyze appropriate data in order to extract new values" (Figure 15). Thereby the values for all participating stakeholders are outlined once more, whilst an answer on Quemey's own role is given as well. The heading of new values leads to Quemey's USP: they empower all parties involved to create new values – regarding consumers, new value emerges from making better use of their time by sharing data in exchange for incentives, and for producers and partners new value is jointly realized by co-creation. Simultaneously, they reduce uncertainty, because of the control options for consumers with whom they share their data, and because of the guidance for producers and partners in a world of digital disruption and unlimited technological possibilities. *"In this new world, speed of learning has become the new unfair advantage"* (Maurya, Continuous Innovation. The way we build products has fundamentally changed, 2017, S. 4) – this is what Ash Maurya states in "Continuous Innovation", where he elucidates how today's solution to a problem is not a product anymore, but rather a BM (Maurya, Continuous Innovation. The way we build products has fundamentally changed, 2017, S. 3). This unfair advantage is also what Quemey needs to outperform their competitors and conquer their market. Next to this, Quemey's mission statement was adopted from their PVC.

It remains the third layer with corresponding **strategies** to realize the above positioning. In terms of resources, Quemey should grow their entire business, as sketched before. Proceeding with the business case aspect, this is where the need to specify a monetization and pricing model and make it work with a certain willingness to pay is anchored. Ultimately, for Quemey's market-based strategy, a central focus topic is to approach and convince new contacts with the help of appropriate marketing, such as the definition of targeted measures and communication channels. Finally,

Quemey's individual solutions from co-creation could even establish lock-in effects, encouraging platform participants to stay with Quemey.

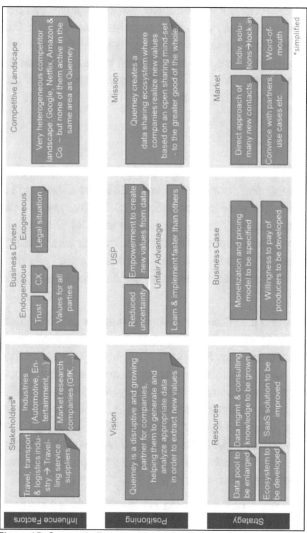

Figure 15: Quemey's Future-oriented Strategy Design
Source: own representation of the author based on (Walter, Lohse, & Guzman, Platform Innovation Kit, 2017, S. 20); again, the size of the stickers does not represent any weighting or emphasis

One side note remains concerning the entire BM elaboration process: the listed elements in the canvases are neither free from overlaps nor exhaustive, meaning it cannot be ruled out that each and every single helpful possibility is listed. Instead, the most relevant aspects are named, and they have been confirmed as such by Quemey's founders. In the sense of a pragmatic research objective, this focus on the most important makes the recommendations manageable, whereas a holistic enumeration of all germane points would be overwhelmingly complex.

3.4.3 Prioritization

"*Prioritization at a strategic and operational level is often the difference between success and failure*" (Nieto-Rodriguez, 2016, S. 2). Despite an initial concentration was made already, the sketched canvases offer a confusingly huge number of recommendations. But what to do first when actually starting the implementation? Due to a lack of resources, particularly time, capacity, manpower and money, a sequence for the described recommendations is needed.

The challenge is to define a prioritized sequence in a systematical and scientific standards complying way, but at the same time to do so in a pragmatic, not overengineered manner. For this reason, a simple matrix representation was chosen, since it combines a scoring model with the subsequent visualization in form of an **Action Priority Matrix** (APM). The APM is a "*simple visual tool that prioritizes a group of ideas, solutions or actions across two dimensions: effort and impact*" (Morin, 2017, S. 1). Whilst effort is associated with the required input factors (costs, time, resources, organizational, legal barriers etc.) to realize an idea, impact depicts the striven effects of the idea's implementation (Morin, 2017, S. 1).

Operationally, an APM is prepared by creating a table with all potential activities, equipped with two columns – one for effort, one for impact – and each activity is rated in these two categories. The two rating scores act as coordinates that help to plot the actions in the APM visualization in step two. The APM itself is divided in four quadrants, representing the prioritization categories: "No Brainers", "Major Projects", "Small Quick Wins" and "Not Worth It" (Morin, 2017, S. 2).

For Quemey, this **process** looks as follows: at first, all potential activities for Quemey are extracted from the above depictions. In order to do so in a structured way, the posed BM creation formula (Figure 12) with all relevant input findings (empirical validation, challenges and perspectives) shall act as starting point. Each input finding is equipped with a proposed solution, which was developed in the course of Quemey's future-oriented BM derivation. Simultaneously, this assures that all posed challenges and needs for action could be cured with the present analysis, which approves that all goals could be met. Afterwards, the ranking regarding effort and impact is executed, showing that certain input findings (or their solutions) do either exist twice or that they are cured already, to the effect that they are excluded from the later APM visualization. In such cases, a short comment provides an explanation and the item itself is strikethrough.

In the same sense as for the BM framework selection in chapter 2.3.3, one could argue that the rating is subjective to a certain extent. This may hold true, but is tried to be reduced to a minimum by providing a short reasoning for each rating in the comments' column. The entire assessment is presented in Table 7

Table 7. Not only does it show that all input factors could be endowed with corresponding solutions, but it also exhibits a certain consolidation process, summarizing similar solutions that cure different problems in a common major action field. Lastly, the APM in Figure 16 presents these **major action fields**, expressing what is recommended for Quemey to put most focus on. It shows that Quemey's two founders should concentrate a large part of their energy on identifying and transporting values for all addressed parties, since this will enable them to approach new producers or to win new consumers. This value identification can take up concrete suggestions and use cases from the expert interviews, like service chain improvements when travelling for example. Simultaneously, Quemey needs to realize their market- and resource-based strategies, as suggested in the platform strategy canvas (Figure 15), to be able to actually deliver their promises. Amongst other things, e.g. the development of a survey app was identified as helpful, since it bundles all desired consumer functionalities in one interface and thereby contributes to the persuasion of more consumers to take part in Quemey's surveys even repeatedly. Lastly, two general factors decide whether a challenge can be mastered: the challenge character itself, and the people who solve it with their skills and knowledge (Eckmann, Dreller, & von Kohout, 2017, S. 28). Thus, Quemey should continuously expand their knowledge in the domains of business, IT and legal topics.

Whereas the above topics represent candidates for major projects, two **no brainers** could be found as well. To realize a self-sustaining business case, Quemey needs to monetize their services, which necessitates a monetization model including the definition of a pricing model and the concurrent development of a certain willingness to pay regarding the priced parties. This is considered an activity that requires brainpower and time only, so it is highly recommended that Quemey's founders invest their time for a first monetization model draft. The same counts for the specification of a concrete service design, which would sharpen Quemey's value proposition and thus facilitate an even stronger performance and appearance in negotiations. If after all these measures there is still **time and manpower left**, Quemey could conduct an environment analysis to understand the changes in their surrounding even better. Since this is estimated to be very time-intense with indirect results only, it is clearly deprioritized.

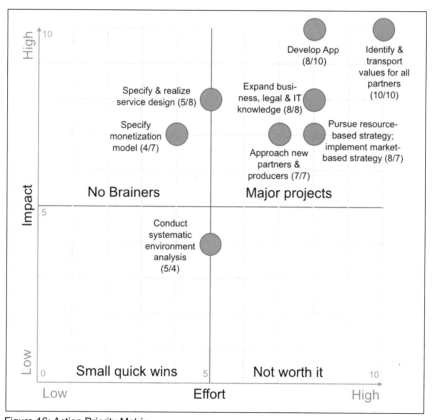

Figure 16: Action Priority Matrix
Source: own representation of the author based on the rating from Table 7

Table 7: Implementation Activity Prioritization

Source	No	Input Finding	Solution Activity	Effort	Impact	Comment
Empiric Validation	1	High general user acceptance identified	Keep pursuing business idea	∅	∅	Yes or now question: go on or stop
	2	Personalized rewards and survey topics preferred	Develop App with preference collection as well as survey topic & reward matching	8	10	Requires IT invest, but great effect on CX
	3	Potential for service improvement & CX recognized	Transport as value for producers, partners and consumers	∅	∅	Included as value in 14 and 18
Current Challenges	4	Not enough stakeholders	Approach new producers & partners (as suggested in platform value canvas) & convince them to join Quemey's ecosystem	7	7	Time-intense but very effective if successful
	5	Poor understanding regarding stakeholders	Approach new producers & partners (as suggested in platform value canvas) & improve Quemey's understanding of their world	7	7	Time-intense but very effective if successful
	6	No powerful values transported	Identify & transport values for each party	∅	∅	see 14 & 18
	7	No clear transaction design specified	Specify & realize service design incl. concrete transaction design for all involved parties (see platform service canvas)	5	8	Requires time & brainpower only, but enables clear service proposition
	8	No data sharing in mission statement included	Anchor data sharing approach in vision & mission	∅	∅	Already done (see Figure 21 & Figure 23)
	9	Environment challenge	Conduct systematic environment analysis, particular regarding competitors & trends	5	4	Requires much time, indirect effects only

	10	Implementation challenge	Pursue resource-based strategy (see strategy canvas)	8	7	Requires invest, but crucial to deliver
			~~Realize business case~~	Ø	Ø	~~see 13~~
			Implement market-based strategy (see strategy canvas)	8	7	Requires invest, but brings more participants
	11	~~Scaling challenge~~	~~Scale data base and business~~	Ø	Ø	~~Will become relevant after implementation~~
	12	Uniqueness challenge	Expand business & IT knowledge to learn and implement faster than others, to strengthen differentiation	8	8	Continuous effort, but crucial for all other activities
			~~Grow to increase platform power~~	Ø	Ø	~~Included in 16~~
	13	Business case challenge	Specify monetization model incl. pricing model and development of willingness to pay	4	7	Requires time & brain only, but enables to make money
Future Perspectives	14	Show partners / producers value from data	Identify and transport values, e.g.: ▪ Service & product improvements possible ▪ Resulting in customer satisfaction & loyalty, financial & economic success, even publicity & reputation (partners) ▪ Constituting a competitive advantage	10	10	Permanent activity, but a 100% success-determining
	15	~~Increase partner / producer contacts~~	~~Approach new producers & partners~~	Ø	Ø	~~Included in 4 & 5~~

16	Grow data base and business	Expand business & IT knowledge to learn and implement faster than others, in order to grow	8	8	Continuous effort, but crucial for all other activities
17	Eliminate barriers for producers/ partners who demand data (technological & contractual uncertainties)	Expand business & IT knowledge to reduce uncertainty with excellent consulting services	8	8	Continuous effort, but crucial for all other activities
		~~And specify service design~~	Ø	Ø	~~included in 7~~
18	Show benefits for consumers from sharing their data	Identify and transport values, e.g.: • Make better use of time • Possibility to influence services & products • Interesting & entertaining survey topics • Attractive rewards	10	10	Permanent activity, but a 100% success-determining
19	~~Personalize rewards & survey topics~~	~~Develop App with respective features~~	Ø	Ø	~~Included in 2~~
20	Establish trust	Develop App with incl. transparent control option concerning own data sharing permissions	8	10	Requires IT invest, but great effect on CX
21	~~Reach more consumers~~	~~Implement market-based strategy~~	Ø	Ø	~~Included in 10~~
22	Eliminate barriers for consumers (effort to participate & intransparent conditions)	Develop App with convenient, attractive design and gamification elements	8	1	Requires IT invest, but great effect on CX
		~~And specify service design~~	Ø	Ø	~~included in 7~~
23	Show value for producers/ partners from sharing their data	Identify and transport sharing values, e.g.: • Possibility to improve services & products	10	10	Permanent activity, but a 100% success-determining

			• Resulting in customer satisfaction & loyalty, financial & economic success			
	24	~~Increase partner / producer contacts~~	~~Approach new producers & partners~~	⊘	⊘	~~Included in 4 & 5~~
	25	Encourage a sharing mindset	Approach new producers & partners (as suggested in platform value canvas) and encourage sharing mind-set by transporting values and reducing uncertainties	7	7	Time-intense but very effective if successful
	26	Eliminate barriers for producers/ partners regarding data sharing (expected weakening, legal, techn. & contractual uncertainties)	~~Show that value from sharing is greater than weakening~~	⊘	⊘	~~Included in 23~~
			Expand business, legal & IT knowledge to • Reduce uncertainties	8	8	Continuous effort, but crucial for all other activities

Source: own representation of the author based on previous analyses

4 Conclusion

4.1 Discussion

Altogether, many results have been produced, but it remains to clarify to what extent they are valid and comply scientific requirements. Hence, the following section will critically reflect and discuss the entire knowledge production process.

As far as **criticism on the choice of methodologies** is concerned, each utilized method shows both advantages and disadvantages when contemplated on its own. Partly, these have been investigated in the course of the methodology introduction in 2.3. Regarding case studies, for instance, the scientific community discusses whether they are accepted as scientific method at all. And even if so, one could state they are rather appropriate for theory testing than for theory building (Dul & Hak, 2008, S. 7). Other than that, Walter's platform BM framework was published only recently, to the effect that it is neither well-known nor a commonly accepted research tool yet. Or there are opinions that e.g. expert interviews are not sufficient for valid conclusions when applied on their own (Kaiser, 2014, S. V). Picking up all these thoughts, a multi-method research design was intended to cure the individual methodologies' weaknesses by using them in joint interplay.

Another aspect that is to be treated is **criticism regarding the chosen methods' application** in the present research project. Presumably one could argue that

- the postulated key design principles are not verified as goal-oriented
- the case study was conceptualized too unstructeredly
- Walter's chosen platform BM was completed with confusingly many items
- airport interviews cannot be qualitative when evaluated in percentages
- the survey questionnaire was not tested sufficiently before its go live
- the scenarios were developed unidirectional and not verified
- that a "post it light version" qualitative content analysis is not scientific enough

© Springer Fachmedien Wiesbaden GmbH, part of Springer Nature 2018
A. Dreller, *Creating Value from Data Sharing*, Informationsmanagement in Theorie und Praxis, https://doi.org/10.1007/978-3-658-23276-4_4

– to list just one example for each applied method. All these aspects may be criticized from an academic point of view, but have been deprioritized in favour of the postulated meta goal to deliver the promised solution in a pragmatic and realistically feasible way.

Nonetheless, the entire research design with its described interplay of methodologies was selected **subjectively** to a certain degree. Some instruments do even have a subjective character themselves, as e.g. pointed out for the scenario analysis (see 2.3.6). Equally, the chosen scenario names or the appointed rating scores were ideas of the author. Accordingly, they can be called subjectively selected as well, even though a systematic reasoning was provided to substantiate the respective train of thoughts. However, each thought and each idea that is produced by a human brain has a subjective character to a certain extent, which cannot be negated, but analyzed with appropriate theories and tests – like it was done in the present case. When doing so, there might come a point that indicates the chosen research design is not sufficiently capable to bring the aspired results. In this case, it is essential for researchers to adjust their original plan. This became obvious after all recommended canvases from Walter's platform BM framework were completed and there was a confusingly high amount of recommendations, partly even overlapping. Hence, a prioritization was added, to assure that Quemey does not get confused, but manages to focus on the most relevant.

Regarding the actual **content-wise validity** of all findings, ultimately only reality can show whether the proposed recommendations bring progress for Quemey – or whether they even hold true in general when transferred to similar companies.

4.2 Summary

This project started with the overarching research objective to draw up a future-oriented BM design for Quemey that resonates with their aspired data sharing approach ("what" dimension), and to do so in a pragmatic and realistically feasible manner to pave the way for its implementation ("how" dimension). In combination, these two aspects should answer the underlying research question how a future-oriented BM can look like that creates new values from data sharing.

Now this project closes with an attempt to put the **quintessence** of the broad range of obtained findings on this huge topic area into a nutshell. After scoping the research objective by defining a concrete action plan, the **theory section** helped to find a common understanding on relevant terminology. Moreover, it pointed out the massive transformative power of today's technological progress, and the outstanding meaning of data for our economy. But to actually unleash the value inherent in data, they need to be transformed and interpreted, which is only possible with the critical prerequisite of data access. This is where data sharing becomes relevant, necessary to combine different data sources and extract (more) value. In face of the mentioned technological progress, there are possibilities available to do so technically. But considering the expected benefits for common wealth or monetization opportunities from data sharing, embedded in related phenomena of the sharing economy and new platform businesses, it is the question whether these benefits are actually recognized yet. Whilst in **research** data sharing is estimated very beneficial for the progress of science, there are practical challenges, mostly about lacking standards, rules, agreements and conditions. Contrarily, examples from the **business world** showed that companies still need to recognize the value emerging from data sharing, exceeding the loss from opening up sensitive information. Here, the realization of data sharing faces minor technological challenges (particularly regarding data evaluation and application) but again major challenges when commercial agreements are concerned.

The **case study part** took these findings and mirrored them against the real-world example of the startup Quemey. A multi-method research design, compiled by customers interviews, a subsequent online survey, expert interviews, and a scenario analysis helped to describe Quemey's current BM and to develop a future-oriented one, using Walter's platform innovation kit as framework.

For their **current BM**, Quemey's central vision is to make better use of air passengers' most valuable resource, namely their time. Apart from that, most other aspects are vaguely defined only, with surveys and rewards for air passengers or data for producers of surveys named as most important ones. Notwithstanding, the empiric validation showed an extremely high level of confirmation of Quemey's basic idea, but also a wish for personalized topics and rewards.

Based on these interview and survey findings, and augmented by insights from expert interviews, Quemey's current **challenges** were composed subsequently. Along the dimensions of Quemey's current BM, it is a key task to better convince and understand their stakeholders, and to refine the current values, for them to become powerful and persuasive. Equally, the transaction design needs to be concretized, and Quemey's overall vision should integrate data sharing in the future. In addition, general challenges regarding an environment analysis, implementation, scaling, uniqueness and a self-sustaining business case were discovered. On top of that, a scenario analysis revealed future perspectives in which both data demand and supply need to be stimulated, particularly by showing strong values, growing Quemey's business towards a powerful monopolist position, and eliminating interfering influences such as technological, contractual and legal uncertainties or data privacy concerns – in line with the findings from theory.

All these input factors could then be **condensed in Quemey's future-oriented business model**. It now pursues the key vision of creating a data sharing ecosystem, and compiles powerful values that address underlying motivational structures of the involved parties, for instance entertainment for consumers or long-term corporate success for producers and partners. To make a first step towards implementation, Walter's service and strategy

canvases were compiled. Since a huge number of recommendations remained in total, a prioritization condensed the most important aspects,
which are again and above all the further refinement of strong values, the
continued development of Quemey's resources and marketing (including
a survey app), the enhancement of Quemey's knowledge as precondition
for all other actions, and lastly to pursue new contacts.

Finally, this confirms that the **overarching objective was achieved**. Both
in its "what" dimension, as just portrayed, and in its "how" dimension, since
not only a static BM description was given, but also prioritized next steps.
Moreover, the idea of pragmatism was systematically anchored in the entire research design, and is therefore expected to have delivered pragmatic
results. The created BM can also be called future-oriented, since it is based
on information and – once grown – highly scalable, which will make it an
ExO if the designed plan works out.

What became obvious as well: the deeper a researcher explores a certain
topic area and the more findings this brings, the greater the number of new
questions that simultaneously appear. These open questions are not understood as research gaps, but rather as gifts, which encourage further
investigation and scientific progress. Thus, the outlook will now deal with
open issues and future topics.

4.3 Outlook

As stated in the discussion section: only reality will show whether the recommended actions bring Quemey sustainable success. Correspondingly,
it remains exciting whether all points can be taken up and if so, which impact they will have. Many **open issues** emerge from what was suggested
to do next. How exactly does Quemey translate the identified motivational
values for all involved platform parties into actual use cases? Will it go into
the proposed direction of e.g. service and CX improvement, and can other
ideas from the conducted expert interviews help? How will they communicate them in the most effective way? How can they identify and reach new

attractive platform participants? How can they scale their business to become a major platform player, developing towards a monopolist position, to conquer the travelling value chain with their platform ecosystem after all? The only way to find answers is to accompany Quemey when turning the advised next steps into reality.

A very interesting aspect is whether the obtained findings hold true for the specific case of Quemey only, or whether they can be **transferred** to similar or even incomparable (platform) companies. Initiating according investigations with other cases might answer this question, and beyond that, it might even allow for refinements on Walter's platform BM framework, or lead to an entirely new platform model, that manages to capture the identified dynamics more suitably.

"Digital disruption has only just begun" (Nanterme, 2016, S. 1). Digitalization is not only omnipresent and a major topic on each CEO's agenda, it is also expected to stay so and to become even more important in the near future. One last time, this underpins the **outstanding relevance** of the examined research topic. Everything that can be connected, will be connected (Höttges, 2016, S. 5), hence it is crucial to learn how to convert these new data masses into new sources of value. Also for Quemey this brings excellent future prospects. With enhanced possibilities of data collection, they might be able to augment the data they gather from surveys by other sources of passive data collection. Can we imagine that one day our smartphone, our smart watch, our connected car, our smart home equipment and all other connected devices in our life will know everything about us – and share their knowledge with companies, such as Quemey

References

Abolhassan, F. (2016). Digitalisierung als Ziel - Cloud als Motor. In F. Abolhassan (Ed.), *Was treibt die Digitalisierung? Warum kein Weg an der Cloud vorbeiführt* (pp. 15-26). Wiesbaden: Springer Gabler.

Aghamanoukjan, A., Buber, R., & Michael, M. (2009). Qualitative Interviews. In R. Buber, & H. Holzmüller (Eds.), *Qualitative Marktforschung. Konzepte - Methoden - Analysen* (pp. 415-436). Wiesbaden: Gabler | GWV Fachverlage GmbH.

Amit, R., & Zott, C. (2001). Value Creation in E-Business. *Strategic Management Journal, 22*(6-7), 493-520.

Anderson, J. C. (1995). Relationships in Business Markets: Exchange Episodes, Value Creation, and Their Empirical Assessment. *Journal of the Academy of Marketing Science, 23*(4), 346-350.

Augustin, S. (1990). *Information als Wettbewerbsfaktor: Informationslogistik - Herausforderung an das Management.* Zürich: Industrielle Organisation.

Baan, P., & Homburg, R. (2013). Information Productivity: An Introduction to Enterprise Information Management. In P. Baan (Ed.), *Enterprise Information Management. When Information Becomes Inspiration* (pp. 1-42). De Meern: Springer.

Barbará, D., & Clifton, C. (1993). Information brokers: Sharing Knowledge in a Heterogeneous Distributed System. *International Conference on Database and Expert Systems Applications.* Prague.

Basulto, D. (2012, 03 30). *The Washington Post.* Retrieved 12 10, 2017, from The new #Fail: Fail fast, fail early and fail often: https://www.washingtonpost.com/blogs/innovations/post/the-new-fail-fail-fast-fail-early-and-fail-

© Springer Fachmedien Wiesbaden GmbH, part of Springer Nature 2018
A. Dreller, *Creating Value from Data Sharing*, Informationsmanagement in Theorie und Praxis, https://doi.org/10.1007/978-3-658-23276-4

often/2012/05/30/gJQAKA891U_blog.html?utm_term=.fca04f790
683

Bode, C. (2014). *Die Nutzung von Marktforschungsinformationen. Eine empirische Untersuchung zur Bedeutung der Unternehmensmarktforschung.* Wiebaden: Springer Gabler.

Bodendorf, F. (2006). *Daten- und Wissensmanagement* (2nd ed.). Berlin / Heidelberg: Springer-Verlag.

Bogner, A., Littig, B., & Menz, W. (2014). *Interviews mit Experten. Eine praxisorientierte Einführung.* Wiesbaden: Springer Fachmedien.

Bohlman, J., Kletzel, J., & Terry, B. (2017, 03 24). *2017 Commercial Aviation Trends.* Retrieved 12 13, 2017, from Strategy&: https://www.strategyand.pwc.com/media/file/2017-Commercial-Aviation-Trends.pdf

Bombardier. (2017, 09 12). *Five Key Trends Affecting Commercial Aviation for the Next 20 Years.* Retrieved 12 13, 2017, from Aviation Week Network: http://aviationweek.com/commercial-aviation/five-key-trends-affecting-commercial-aviation-next-20-years

Bowcott, H. (2017, 11). *Powered by data, driven by people: The travel sector's future.* Retrieved 12 13, 2017, from McKinsey Travel, Transport & Logistics: https://www.mckinsey.com/industries/travel-transport-and-logistics/our-insights/powered-by-data-driven-by-people-the-travel-sectors-future

Bratianu, C. (2018). The Crazy New World of the Sharing Economy. In E.-M. Vatamanescu, & F. M. Pînzaru (Eds.), *Knowledge Management in the Sharing Economy. Cross-Sectoral Insights into the Future of Competitive Advantage* (pp. 3-18). Cham: Springer International Publishing AG.

Châlons, C., & Dufft, N. (2016). Die Rolle der IT als Enabler für Digitalisierung. In F. Abolhassan (Ed.), *Was treibt die*

Digitalisierung? Warum an der Cloud kein Weg vorbeiführt (pp. 27-37). Wiesbaden: Springer Gabler.

Christensen, C. M. (1997). *The Innovator's Dilemma. When New Technologies Cause Great Companies to Fail.* Boston: Harvard Business School Press.

Christensen, G. E., & Methlie, L. B. (2003). Value Creation in eBusiness: Exploring the Impacts of Internet-Enabled Business Conduct. *16th Bled eCommerce Conference eTransformation.* Bled, Slovenia.

Clark, T., Osterwalder, A., & Pigneur, Y. (2012). *Business Model You: A One-Page Method For Reinventing Your Career* . Hoboken: John Wiley & Sons, Inc. .

Clement, R., & Schreiber, D. (2016). *Internet-Ökonomie. Grundlagen und Fallbeispiele der vernetzten Wirtschaft* (3rd ed.). Berlin / Heidelberg: Springer Gabler.

Cole, T. (2010). *Unternehmen 2020. Das Internet war erst der Anfang.* München: Carl Hanser Verlag.

Cowden, P. D. (2013). *Neustart. Das Ende der Wirtschaft wie wir sie kennen. Ab jetzt zählt der Mensch.* München: Ariston Verlag in der Verlagsgruppe Random House GmbH.

Decker, R., & Wagner, R. (2002). *Marketingforschung: Methoden und Modelle zur Bestimmung des Käuferverhaltens.* München: Moderne Industrie.

Deelmann, T., & Loos, P. (2003). *Visuelle Methoden zur Darstellung von Geschäftsmodellen – Methodenvergleich, Anforderungsdefinition und exemplarischer Visualisierungsvorschlag. Paper 13.* Mainz: Working Papers of the Research Group Information Systems & Management, Universität Mainz, Prof. Dr. Peter Loos.

Dehnhard, I. (2014). *Data Management & Data Sharing: Eine Einführung.* Trier: Leibniz-Institut für Psychologische Information und Dokumentation (ZPID).

Diamandis, P. H. (2017). Vorwort. In *Exponentielle Organisationen. Das Konstruktionsprinzip für die Transformation von Unternehmen im Informationszeitalter* (pp. V-VIII). München: Verlag Franz Vahlen GmbH.

Dul, J., & Hak, T. (2008). Aims and Overview of this Book. In J. Dul, & T. Hak (Eds.), *Case Study Methodology in Business Research* (pp. 3-18). Oxford / Burlington: Elsevier Ltd.

Eckartz, S. M., Hofman, W. J., & Van Veenstra, A. F. (2014). A Decision Model for Data Sharing. *Electronic Government. 13th IFIP WG 8.5 International Conference, EGOV 2014.* (pp. 253-264). Dublin: Springer.

Eckmann, D., Dreller, A., & von Kohout, L. (2017). Interne Beratungen - Herausforderungen, Geschäftsmodelle, Zukunftsperspektiven. In T. Deelmann, & D. M. Ockel (Eds.), *Handbuch der Unternehmensberatung* (pp. 4651/1-32). Berlin: Erich Schmidt Verlag.

Ematinger, R. (2018). *Von der Industrie 4.0 zum Geschäftsmodell 4.0. Chancen der digitalen Transformation.* Wiesbaden: Springer Gabler.

Ferilli, S. (2011). *Automatic Digital Document Processing and Management. Problems, Algorithms and Techniques.* London: Springer-Verlag London Limited.

Fleischer, D. (2017, 11 28). Expert Interview Dennis Fleischer. (A. Dreller, Interviewer)

Flint, D. J., Woodruff, R. B., & Fisher Gardial, S. (1997). Customer Value Change in Industrial Marketing Relationships. A Call for New Strategies and Research. *Industrial Marketing Management, 26*(2), 163-175.

Foley, J. T., & Harðardótti, S. (2016). Creative Axiomatic Design. *26th CIRP Design Conference. Procedia CIRP 50 (2016)*, (pp. 240-245). Stockholm.

Foscht, T., Angerer, T., & Swoboda, B. (2009). Mixed Methods. Systematisierung von Untersuchungsdesigns. In R. Buber, & H. H. Holzmüller (Eds.), *Qualitative Marktforschung. Konzepte - Methoden - Analysen* (2nd ed., pp. 247-259). Wiesbaden: Gabler | GWV Fachverlage GmbH.

Gadatsch, A. (2012). *Grundkurs Geschäftsprozessmanagement. Methoden und Werkzeuge für die IT-Praxis: Eine Einführung für Studenten und Praktiker* (7th ed.). Wiesbaden: Vieweg+Teubner Verlag | Springer Fachmedien.

Gansky, L. (2010). *The Mesh. Why the Future of Business is Sharing.* New York: Portfolio Penguin.

Gassmann, O., Frankenberger, K., & Csik, M. (2013). *Geschäftsmodelle entwickeln. 55 innovative Konzepte mit dem St. Galler Business Model Navigator.* München: Carl Hanser Verlag.

Giese, P. (2017, 11 29). *IOTA eröffnet Daten-Marktplatz.* Retrieved 12 06, 2017, from BTC-Echo. Bitcoin & Blockchain Pioneers: https://www.btc-echo.de/iota-eroeffnet-daten-marktplatz/amp/

Goldhammer, K. (2013). Teilen, tauschen, leihen: Wie Shareconomy dank Smartphone und mobilem Internet immer weiter um sich greift. *Digitaltrends LfM, 7*(2), 4-7.

Gottlieb, J., & Rifai, K. (2017, 12). *Fueling growth through data monetization.* Retrieved 12 06, 2017, from McKinsey & Company: https://www.mckinsey.com/business-functions/mckinsey-analytics/our-insights/fueling-growth-through-data-monetization?cid=other-eml-alt-mip-mck-oth-1712

Greenberg, E., Hirt, M., & Smit, S. (2017). The Global Forces Inspiring a New Narrative of Progress. *McKinsey Quarterly, 34*(2), 32-52.

Günther, E. (no release date specified). *Action Sheets.* Retrieved 12 12, 2017, from Technische Universität Dresden. Companies and Climate Change - An Informational website of the Chair of Environmental Management and Accounting:

http://www.unternehmen-
klimawandel.de/dokumente/massnahmen/Die_Methode_Szenari
oanalyse.pdf

Heitger, B., & Serfass, A. (2015). *Unternehmensentwicklung. Wissen,
Wege, Werkzeuge für morgen.* Stuttgart: Schäffer-Poeschel
Verlag.

Hindle, T. (2008). *Guide to Management Ideas and Gurus.* London:
Profile Books Ltd.

Hinrichs, H. (2002, 01 17). *Datenqualitätsmanagement in Data
Warehouse-Systemen (Thesis PhD).* Oldenburg: Universität
Oldenburg . Retrieved from http://oops.uni-
oldenburg.de/279/1/309.pdf

Hinterhuber, H. H. (2015). *Strategische Unternehmensführung. Das
Gesamtmodell für nachhaltige Wertsteigerung* (9th ed.). Berlin:
Erich Schmidt Verlag.

Hoffmeister, C. (2015). *Digital Business Modelling. Digitale
Geschäftsmodelle entwickeln und strategisch verankern.*
München: Carl Hanser Verlag.

Holstein, W. K., & Campell, D. R. (2009). Efficient and Effective Strategy
Implementation: the Next Source of Competitive Advantage. In R.
Berndt (Ed.), *Weltwirtschaft 2010. Trends und Strategien* (pp. 57-
70). Berlin, Heidelberg: Springer-Verlag.

Höttges, T. (2016). Geleitwort. In F. Abolhassan (Ed.), *Was treibt die
Digitalisierung? Warum kein Weg an der Cloud vorbeiführt* (pp. 5-
8). Wiesbaden: Springer Gabler.

Ismail, S., Malone, M. S., & Van Geest, Y. (2014). *Exponentielle
Organisation. Das Konstruktionsprinzip für die Transformation
von Unternehmen im Informationszeitalter.* München: Verlag
Franz Vahlen.

Jans, R., & Dittrich, K. (2008). A Review of Case Studies in Business Research. In J. Dul, & T. Hak (Eds.), *Case Study Methodology in Business Research* (pp. 19-29). Oxford / Burlington: Elsevier Ltd.

Johnson, M. W. (2010). *Seizing the White Space. Business Model Innovation for Growth and Renewal.* Boston, Massachusetts: Harvard Business Press.

Kaiser, R. (2014). *Qualitative Experteninterviews. Konzeptionelle Grundlagen und praktische Durchführung.* Wiesbaden: Springer Fachmedien.

Kerth, K., Asum, H., & Stich, V. (2015). *Die besten Strategietools in der Praxis. Welche Werkzeuge brauche ich wann? Wie wende ich sie an? Wo liegen die Grenzen?* München: Carl Hanser Verlag.

Kim, T.-Y., Kim, E., Park, J., & Hwang, J. (2014). The Faster-Accelerating Digital Economy. In T.-Y. Kim, & A. Heshmati (Eds.), *Economic Growth: The New Perspectives for Theory and Policy* (pp. 163-191). Berlin/ Heidelberg: Springer-Verlag.

Kishore, R., & McLean, E. R. (2002). The Next Generation Enterprise: A CIO Perspective on the Vision, its Impacts, and Implementation Challenges. *Information Systems Frontiers, 4*(1), 121-138.

Kraus, S., & Giselbrecht, C. (2015). Shareconomy: Das disruptive Geschäftsmodell des Teilens. *Zeitschrift für KMU und Entrepreneurship, 63*(1), 77-93.

Krumm, J. M., Sabin, J., & Clark, D. (1999). Integrating Legacy Systems: The Information Broker. *Journal of Digital Imaging, 12*(2), 201-202.

Kurzweil, R. (2001, 03 07). *The Law of Accelerating Returns.* Retrieved 12 02, 2017, from Kurzweil Accelerating Intelligence : http://www.kurzweilai.net/the-law-of-accelerating-returns

Latham, G. P. (2001). The reciprocal effects of science on practice: Insights from the practice and science of goal setting. *Canadian Psychology/Psychologie Canadienne, 42*(1), 1-11.

Maurya, A. (2012). *Running Lean. Iterate from Plan A to a Plan That Works* (2nd ed.). Sebastopol: O'Reilly.

Maurya, A. (2017, 12 15). *Continuous Innovation. The way we build products has fundamentally changed.* Retrieved 12 19, 2017, from Blog.Leanstack.com: https://blog.leanstack.com/continuous-innovation-c004d46a9250

Mayring, P. (2010). Qualitative Inhaltsanalyse. In G. Mey, & K. Mruck (Eds.), *Handbuch Qualitative Forschung in der Psychologie* (pp. 601-613). Wiesbaden: VS Verlag für Sozialwissenschaften | Springer Fachmedien Wiesbaden GmbH.

Mayring, P., & Brunner, E. (2009). Qualitative Inhaltsanalyse. In R. Buber, & H. H. Holzmüller (Eds.), *Qualitative Marktforschung. Konzepte - Methoden - Analysen* (2nd ed., pp. 669-680). Wiesbaden: Gabler | GWV Fachverlage GmbH.

Mayring, P., & Fenzl, T. (2014). Qualitative Inhaltsanalyse. In N. Baur, & J. Blasius (Eds.), *Handbuch Methoden der empirischen Sozialforschung* (pp. 543-558). Wiesbaden: Springer Fachmedien.

Mbuagbaw, L., Foster, G., Cheng, J., & Thabane, L. (2017). Challenges to complete and useful data sharing. *Trials, 71*(18), 1-3.

Mehrjerdi, Y. Z. (2010). Enterprise resource planning: risk and benefit analysis. *Business Strategy Series, 11*(5), 308-324.

Mey, G., & Mruck, K. (2010). Interviews. In G. Mey, & K. Mruck (Eds.), *Handbuch Qualitative Forschung in der Psychologie* (pp. 423-435). Wiesbaden: VS Verlag für Sozialwissenschaften | Springer Fachmedien Wiesbaden GmbH.

Meyer, C. B. (2001). A Case in Case Study Methodology. *Field Methods, 13*(4), 329-352.

Moore, G. A. (2005). *Dealing with Darwin. How Great Companies Innovate at Every Phase of Their Evolution.* New York: Portfolio.

Morin, J. (2017, 02 13). *Action Priority Matrix.* Retrieved 12 20, 2017, from LinkedIn: https://www.linkedin.com/pulse/action-priority-matrix-jason-morin

Mühleck, K. H. (2016). Harmonisierung und Standardisierung durch die Cloud. In F. Abolhassan (Ed.), *Was treibt die Digitalisierung? Warum kein Weg an der Cloud vorbei führt* (pp. 129-140). Wiesbaden: Springer Gabler.

Nanterme, P. (2016, 01 17). *Digital disruption has only just begun.* Retrieved 12 28, 2017, from World Economic Forum: https://www.weforum.org/agenda/2016/01/digital-disruption-has-only-just-begun/

Nieto-Rodriguez, A. (2016, 12 13). *Project Management. How to Prioritize Your Company's Projects.* Retrieved 12 20, 2017, from Harvard Busienss Review: https://hbr.org/2016/12/how-to-prioritize-your-companys-projects

Niven, P. R. (2002). *Balanced Scorecard Step-by-Step: Maximizing Performance and Maintaining Results.* New York: John Wiley & Sons, Inc.

Nordlund, M., Kim, S.-G., Tate, D., Lee, T., & Oh, H. (. (2016). Axiomatic Design: Making the Abstract Concrete. *26th CIRP Design Conference, Procedia CIRP 50 (2016)* (pp. 216-221). Stockholm: Elsevier B.V.

Osterwalder, A., & Pigneur, Y. (2010). *Business Model Generation: A Handbook for Visionaries, Game Changers, and Challengers.* Hoboken: John Wiley & Sons, Inc.

Osterwalder, A., Pigneur, I., Bernarda, G., & Smith, A. (2014). *Value Proposition Design: How to Create Products and Services Customers Want.* Hoboken: John Wiley & Sons, Inc.

Park, G.-J. (2007). *Analytic Methods for Design Practice.* London: Springer-Verlag London Limited.

Paunovic, K. (2008). Data Dissemination and Utilization. In W. Kirch
(Ed.), *Encyclopedia of Public Health* (pp. 199-202). New York:
Springer Science+Business Media, LLC.

Piekenbrock, D., & Hennig, A. (2013). *Einführung in die
Volkswirtschaftslehre und Mikroökonomie* (2nd ed.). Berlin/
Heidelberg: Springer-Verlag.

Pleschak, F., & Sabisch, H. (1996). *Innovationsmanagement.* Stuttgart:
Schäffer-Poeschel.

Poeschl, H. (2013). *Strategische Unternehmensführung zwischen
Shareholder-Value und Stakeholder-Value.* Wiesbaden: Springer
Gabler.

Quemey. (no release date specified). *Quemey.* (Quemey GmbH)
Retrieved 11 05, 2017, from https://quemey.de

Ranjan, J. (2008). Business justification with business intelligence. *VINE:
The journal of information and knowledge management systems ,
38*(4), 461-475.

Reinecke, J. (2014). Grundlagen der standardisierten Befragung. In N.
Baur, & J. Blasius (Eds.), *Handbuch Methoden der empirischen
Sozialforschung* (pp. 601-618). Wiesbaden: Springer
Fachmedien.

Richter, C. (2016). *Digital Collaboration and Entrepreneurship - The Role
of Shareeconomy and Crowdsourcing in the Era of Smart City.*
Lappeenranta: Lappeenranta University of Technology.

Richter, C., & Kraus, S. S. (2015). The shareconomy as a precursor for
digital entrepreneurship business models. *International Journal of
Entrepreneurship and Small Business, 25*(1), 18-35.

Ries, E. (2011). *The Lean Startup. How Today's Entrepreneurs Use
Continuous Innovation to Create Radically Successful
Businesses.* New York: Crown Business.

Rogers, D. L. (2017). *Digitale Transformation. Das Playbook. Wie Sie Ihr Unternehmen erfolgreich in das digitale Zeitalter führen und die digitale Disruption meistern.* Frechen: mitp Verlags GmbH.

Sander, A. (2007). 6. Innovieren leicht gemacht ... mit den richtigen Führungskräften und unterstützenden Werkzeugen. In K. Engel, & M. Nippa (Eds.), *Innovationsmanagement. Von der Idee zum erfolgreichen Produkt* (pp. 95-110). Heidelberg: Physica-Verlag.

Schaumberger, K. (2011, 03 20). *Ökonomisches Prinzip.* Retrieved 12 06, 2017, from Existenzgründer Helfer: https://www.existenzgruender-helfer.de/2011/03/20/oekonomisches-prinzip-wirtschaftlichkeitsprinzip/

Scheer, C., Deelmann, T., & Loos, P. (2003). *Geschäftsmodelle und internetbasierte Geschäftsmodelle – Begriffsbestimmung und Teilnehmermodell. Paper 12.* Mainz: Working Papers of the Research Group Information Systems & Management, Universität Mainz, Prof. Dr. Peter Loos.

Scheuch, E. K. (1973). Das Interview in der Sozialforschung. In R. König (Ed.), *Handbuch der empirischen Sozialforschung. Band 2: Grundlegende Methoden und Techniken* (pp. 66-190). München: dtv.

Scheuss, R. (2016). *Handbuch der Strategien. 240 Konzepte der weltbesten Vordenker* (3rd ed.). Frankfurt am Main: Campus Verlag GmbH.

Schütz, B. (2017, 03 25). Interview: Praxisprojekt zu Deinem Startup.

Schütz, B. (2017, 11 21). Interview: Quemey.

Schütz, B., & Fleischer, D. (2017, 09 28). APEX 2017 LONG BEACH. Pitch Deck for Panasonic Avionics. Long Beach, Los Angeles, United States of America: Quemey GmbH.

Schütz, B., & Fleischer, D. (2017, 02 13). Quemey Company Profile. Gau Algesheim, Rhineland-Palatinate, Germany: Quemey GmbH.

Schütz, B., & Fleischer, D. (2017, 10 17). Quemey GmbH. Introduction Emirates. Gau Algesheim, Rhineland-Palatinate, Germany: Quemey GmbH.

Scott, J., & Tesvic, J. (2014). *Implementation.* Retrieved 12 19, 2017, from McKinsey & Company: http://www.mckinsey.com/~/media/McKinsey/dotcom/client_servi ce/Implementation/implementing_change_with_impact_FINAL.as hx

Septer, J. (2013). The Importance of an Enterprise Information Management Strategy. In P. Baan (Ed.), *Enterprise Information Management. When Information Becomes Inspiration* (pp. 43-48). De Meern: Springer.

Sieber, J. E. (1988). Data Sharing. Defining Problems and Seeking Solutions . *Law and Human Behavior, 12*(2), 199-206.

Siemens. (no release date specified). *Siemens Innovation Strategy.* (Siemens) Retrieved 11 29, 2017, from https://www.siemens.com/global/en/home/company/innovation/in novation-strategy.html

Son, Y.-H., Kang, M.-A., Jo, W.-S., Choi, K.-J., & Lee, K.-C. (2014). Platform Design for Data Sharing. In J. J. Park, A. Zomaya, H.-Y. Jeong, & M. Obaidat (Eds.), *Frontier and Innovation in Future Computing and Communications* (pp. 446-452). Dordrecht: Springer Science+Business Media.

Stanley, B., & Stanley, M. (1988). Data Sharing. The Primary Researcher's Perspective. *Law and Human Behaviour, 12*(2), 173-180.

Suh, N. P. (2001). *Axomatic Design: Advances and Applications.* New York / Oxford: Oxford University Press.

Tan, C. N.-L. (2016). Enhancing knowledge sharing and research collaboration among academics: the role of knowledge management. *Higher Education, 71*(4), 525-556.

Telekom Innovation Laboratories. (2017). *Data Analytics*. Retrieved 12
    31, 2017, from Telekom Innovation Laboratories:
    http://www.laboratories.telekom.com/public/Deutsch/Innovation/P
    ages/Data-Analytics.aspx

Tenopir, C., Allard, S., Douglass, K., Aydinoglu, A. U., Wu, L., Read, E., .
    . . Frame, M. (2011). Data Sharing by Scientists: Practices and
    Perceptions. *PLoS ONE, 6*(6), 1-21.

Tiefert, T. (no release date specified). *Strategyzer.com*. (Strategyzer AG)
    Retrieved 11 21, 2017, from
    https://strategyzer.com/canvas/business-model-canvas

Ulbrich Zürni, S. (2004). *Möglichkeiten und Grenzen der
    Szenarioanalyse. Eine Analyse am Beispiel der Schweizer
    Energieplanung.* Stuttgart / Berlin: WiKu-Verlag - Verlag für
    Wissenschaft und Kultur Dr. Stein & Brokamp KG.

Van den Eynden, V. (2017). *Write a Data Management and Sharing Plan.*
    Cancer Research UK. Data Sharing and Management. no city
    specified: UK Data Service.

Van den Eynden, V., Corti, L., Woollard, M., Bishop, L., & Horton, L.
    (2011). *Managing and Sharing Data. Best Practice for
    Researchers.* Colchester: UK Data Archive. University of Essex.

Vissak, T. (2010). Recommendations for Using the Case Study Method in
    International Business Research . *The Qualitative Report, 15*(2),
    370-388.

Voss, C. (2008). Foreword. In J. Dul, & T. Hak (Eds.), *Case Study
    Methodology in Business Research* (pp. XVII-XVIII). Oxford /
    Burlington: Elsevier Ltd.

Wagner, P., & Hering, L. (2014). Online-Befragung. In N. Baur, & J.
    Blasius (Eds.), *Handbuch Methoden der empirischen
    Sozialforschung* (pp. 661-673). Wiesbaden: Springer
    Fachmedien.

Walter, A., Ritter, T., & Gemünden, H. G. (2001). Value Creation in Buyer-Seller Relationships. Theoretical Considerations and Empirical Results from a Supplier's Perspective. *Industrial Marketing Management, 30*(4), 365-377.

Walter, M. (2017, 07 25). Plattform-Geschäftsmodelle verstehen und entwickeln. Berlin: Bitkom-Akademie.

Walter, M. (2017, 12 08). Webinar Plattform Geschäftsmodelle als Königsdisziplin des IoT. no location specified: T-Systems Multimedia Solutions GmbH.

Walter, M., Lohse, M., & Guzman, S. (2017, 04 23). *Platform Innovation Kit.* Retrieved 12 09, 2017, from Download the Platform Innovation Kit: http://www.platforminnovationkit.com/innovate/#downloadkit

Waze. (no release date specified). *Waze.* Retrieved 12 06, 2017, from Waze: https://www.waze.com/en-GB/

Werbach, K., & Hunter, D. (2012). *FOR THE WIN. How GAME THINKING Can Revolutionize Your Business.* Philadelphia: Wharton Digital Press.

Werner, H. (2017). *Supply Chain Management. Grundlagen, Strategien, Instrumente und Controlling* (5th ed.). Wiesbaden: Springer Fachmedien.

Wright, G., & Cairns, G. (2011). *Scenario Thinking. Practical Approaches to the Future.* no city specified: Palgrave Macmillan.

Yin, R. K. (1994). Discovering the Future of the Case Study Method in Evaluation Research. *Evaluation Practice, 15*(3), 283-290.

Yu, Z., Yan, H., & Cheng, T. C. (2001). Benefits of information sharing with supply chain partnerships. *Industrial Management & Data Systems, 101*(3), 114-119.

Zimmermann, B. (2017). Kollege Superhirn. *forum gelb Magazin, 8*(4), 14-19.

Zins, C. (2007). Conceptual Approaches for Defining Data, Information, and Knowledge. *Journal of the American Society for Information Science and Technology, 58*(4), 479-493.

Printed in the United States
By Bookmasters